Body, Mind, and Spirit

*Daily Meditations for Healing
Your Whole Self in Recovery*

Hazelden Publishing
Center City, Minnesota 55012
hazelden.org/bookstore

© 1990 by Hazelden Foundation
All rights reserved. First published 1990 by Parkside Publishing Corporation.
Published by Hazelden Foundation 1994
Printed in the United States of America

ISBN: 978-1-56838-077-3

Editor's notes

In the process of being reissued in 2020, *Body, Mind, and Spirit* has undergone minor editing updates and has been retypeset in the Whitman font family.

This book was formerly titled *Body, Mind, and Spirit: Daily Meditations*.

To the greatest degree possible, the accuracy of quotations and sources has been verified.

This book utilizes phrases from the Twelve Steps, which are from *Alcoholics Anonymous*, 4th ed. (New York: Alcoholics Anonymous World Services, 2001), 59–60.

24 23 22   2 3 4 5 6

COVER DESIGN: PERCOLATOR GRAPHIC DESIGN
INTERIOR DESIGN: TERRI KINNE
TYPESETTING: PERCOLATOR GRAPHIC DESIGN

This book is dedicated to all those who are
healing from the disease of addiction.

JANUARY

*Now that I knew fear, I also knew it was not
permanent. As powerful as it was, its grip on
me would loosen. It would pass.*

— Louise Erdrich

When trouble tumbles down on us, it's easy to become
overwhelmed. We see problems facing us in the future
and mountains of work to do. We look at the past and
see the pain and struggle of addiction. Looking at all
this, we might feel despair. We can't handle it. We want
to run. Our thoughts begin to spin; we feel caught in a
whirlwind. We feel we will break.

Then, softly, we hear the words of our Twelve Step
program: "One day at a time." We find we can slow down
and take a moment to let the peace of our Higher Power
touch us. Now we can take one small step at a time. We
can begin the task before us—doing the next right thing.
By slowing down and taking action, we stop the spinning
and find calm. We find that we can handle the stress of
the moment, and we can be sure this moment will pass.

*Today help me to stay focused on life,
one moment at a time.*

Every exit [is] an entrance somewhere else.
— Tom Stoppard

When life asks us to give up something we value, we are always given a replacement. Our new treasure may be disguised and hard to comprehend at first, but it will come shining through if we have faith.

Life offers us choices: Do we choose to believe that the world is basically friendly—or unfriendly? Do we choose to believe that joy may grow from the depths of pain? Do we believe that life has meaning, that there are lessons to be learned from our darkest days, that growth is possible?

Choosing to develop a positive attitude about the changes and losses of life is like opening a window in April after a long winter. Moving through and out of our grief, we begin to feel a sense of hope and direction. We begin to believe that one day, we will come to live without pain as a constant companion.

Sometimes an ounce of courage is all we can cling to in the midst of personal storms. Our willingness to keep going is the quiet act of faith that takes us to a place where we feel safe to open up and trust again.

Today let me trust that I deserve to be happy.

Should you shield the canyons from the wind-storms you would never see the true beauty of their carvings.

— *Elisabeth Kübler-Ross*

Time teaches us about the twofold connection of suffering and wisdom. For every loss, we've gained something new. We are learning that our pain makes us wise over time, but while we are in its midst we often feel alone and entrapped. We sometimes can make no sense out of our suffering—neither its depth nor its seeming unfairness—and we may even turn our backs on our Higher Power. We've survived the darkness only by stumbling through it each day. But in recovery, we have gradually allowed ourselves to accept comfort from others, and their words help us in times of desolation.

We are learning that some pains can't be healed but instead must be endured until they run their course. Sometimes the only hope we have is the deep knowledge that our Higher Power will give us no more than we can handle today. By learning to let go, we can move forward, endure, and find peace.

Today let me trust that—even though it may feel painful—my recovery has begun.

*Draw from others the lesson
that may profit yourself.*
— Terence

Our Twelve Step program offers us the best education in the world, free of charge. Everybody in recovery has something to teach us, if we'll listen. Each of us has a unique background and set of experiences, problems, and solutions to share. From each other we can learn about recovery and about the world, too. We can hear what it's like to live on the streets, even if we didn't lose everything to addiction. We can learn how others got their families involved in a Twelve Step program of their own. We can learn about the problems we may encounter at work, how to avoid them, and how to solve them. We can hear from someone who has been there, rather than through a relapse, how it feels to be addicted to another substance.

The experience of others gives us a rare chance to broaden our horizons. By considering the experience of another, we can learn how to love ourselves enough to combat hatred, how to triumph over adversity, and how to move forward instead of living in the past. Most important, by listening to others with respect and love, we can learn to truly value other people, even those who are different from us.

*Today help me appreciate the teachings of my
Twelve Step program. Help me continue to learn.*

Making prompt amends is the
fresh air of each new day.
— *Sandra Little*

Today brings us a new hill to climb and a new view from the top. Taking time to reflect about our daily journeys is a challenging adventure in self-discovery. Looking down, we see our past trials and difficulties as lessons to learn from. Letting go of old baggage as we end our day will give us a bright window to open onto tomorrow.

Completing a daily inventory creates a good foundation for living peacefully. Honestly acknowledging the things we have done or said to hurt ourselves or others enables us to say we're sorry and to begin each day with a clean slate and a peaceful heart. As we empty ourselves of regret by making amends to ourselves and others, we make room for the love and comfort of our Higher Power.

Today help me take inventory and
make amends where I need to.

*I am the sole author of the dictionary
that defines me.*
— *Zadie Smith*

When we were drinking or using, our loved ones grieved for us terribly. Just as our addiction damaged us, it also hurt those we love. Now that we are in recovery, we can make amends to those we've harmed, but we can't heal them. This they must do on their own, in their own time.

We are not responsible for another person's behavior, but we are responsible for our own. We got help from many sources, but for each of us, recovery is a personal triumph, our own achievement. No one could make us start, and no one could make us stop. We did that ourselves, and we did it by concentrating only on our own lives. This we must continue to do.

Now we have the best of both worlds: the help and support we need to make progress in our programs and the wonderful feeling of achievement and self-respect that comes from recovery.

*Today help me neither blame others
for my problems nor credit them
for my triumphs.*

Optimism is the faith that leads to
achievement; nothing can be done
without hope and confidence.
— *Helen Keller*

When we're in the midst of a distressing time, it can help to try beginning our days with a positive mental outlook. Simply lifting our heads and looking up and out instead of down can make us feel better. Although we can't spend all our time staring at the sky, we can train ourselves to look for the best in ourselves and others.

Even in the middle of great difficulty or pain, we have choices. We can choose a gloom-and-doom attitude and endlessly replay the thoughts that accompany it. Or we can step back and find one good thing. We may be blinded with pain. The situation may appear hopeless, utterly bleak. But recovery guarantees that we are equal to it, that in our pain there is at least one good thing.

We are the masters of our fate. We can change even the most difficult situations with an attitude of hope and positive expectation. Approaching each day with a hopeful heart will give us a different approach to our troubles.

Today help me find one good thing.
Help me let go of fear and negativity.

*The biggest paradox: To be happy, surrender to
what hurts. Forgiveness isn't a one-time deal. The
need to make peace is ongoing.*

— *Melody Beattie*

Making peace with our losses takes time and trust. When
we were living in the pain of our addiction, we acted in
ways that were heartbreaking to ourselves and others.
But now we have a new choice: we can walk the road
of self-forgiveness and stop punishing ourselves for past
deeds, or we can decide that we don't deserve to feel
good, that clinging to our pain, guilt, and self-loathing
will somehow make up for some of the damage.

Believing our wrongs are too great to be righted leaves
us in a perpetual state of mourning. It's a risk, but we can
choose to believe that change is possible, not all at once
but slowly, "One day at a time."

Believing that we are meant to be happy gives us the
courage to make amends and face our past head-on.
When we take the leap of faith necessary to grieve and
let go of the past, we take back our best selves and the
lives we were meant to live.

*Today give me the strength and the
courage to grieve my losses.*

The smaller the head, the bigger the dream.
— Austin O'Malley

When we were small, we dreamed big dreams. We dreamed of flying to the moon or stopping a mountain lion with our bare hands. Our parents and older siblings humored us, and we knew it. But we also knew we could do these things.

As we grew older, we let go of our childhood dreams. We were told to grow up. We were told to be realistic. We were told in so many ways that dreams don't come true. So many of us stopped dreaming. And we grew up.

When we are overwhelmed with pain and problems, resolution may seem as likely as flying to the moon or stopping a mountain lion with our bare hands.

But now, with help from our Higher Power and Twelve Step program, we're starting to believe in miracles again. We're learning how to recapture our childhood selves, how to let our inner child dream big dreams. We cannot accomplish what we cannot imagine. Dreams give us energy, hope, and the courage to take one more step.

Today help me dream. Remind me that I
cannot accomplish what I cannot imagine.

Preach faith till you have it.
— *Peter Boehler*

A little faith is better than no faith. We need not be free from all doubt to turn our will and our lives over to the care of our Higher Power. No one of us has complete faith, perfect faith. We know only that our sobriety depends on our belief in a Power greater than ourselves.

Clearly, we didn't fare so well on our own. Our addiction controlled us. Now that we admit we are powerless over addiction, we need to find something more powerful than ourselves. We have much to gain; we know this from seeing people at meetings who believe in a Higher Power. We know of the serenity and calm that can come from such belief. We'd like that for ourselves, too.

It's tempting to try to carry all burdens alone. But with all that heavy baggage strapped to our backs, everyone else passes us by, free and light from having left their burdens with a Power greater than themselves. We can find that freedom, too.

Today I'll spend a moment in conscious contact
with my Higher Power even though
my faith isn't perfect yet.

We need to learn to become responsible for sooth-
ing the aches and pains of our own heart, rather
than ask—or expect or demand—that our partner
soothe them for us.

— Resmaa Menakem

People who can be happy and whole when alone are best prepared for being with others. If we need relationships in order to feel worthwhile and complete and special, that's the same as drinking or drugging to feel worthwhile.

Helping ourselves naturally feel good can be hard work. It's easier to create false feelings of self-esteem by attaching ourselves to a substance or another person. But once we've created our own feelings of worth, we can sit back and enjoy intimate relationships without fear of being "discovered," abandoned, or lost in the relationship. These fears can cripple us in our recovery and destroy the very thing we're trying to achieve: satisfying intimate relationships.

If we were giving someone a fine old piece of silver, we would first polish away the tarnish. In recovery, we are polishing ourselves by caring for all parts of ourselves— body, mind, and spirit. Soon we can offer ourselves to another as the fine and valuable people we are.

Today let me enjoy my relationship with myself.

The butterfly becomes only when it's entirely ready.
— *Chinese proverb*

Entirely ready? Do we ever feel entirely ready to do anything? This takes some spiritual support. Once, we put things off as much as we could, as often as we could, whenever we could. Action was not a very familiar concept in our lives. Promises—those came more naturally. In a promise there was no demand involved. In time, broken promises became a trademark of our lives.

But not today. Today, we can make a commitment and keep it. Each day we act more responsibly, more consistently, and get more things done.

As we move through stages of becoming entirely ready, we need to stay more constantly in touch with our Higher Power. Because we are so easily threatened by the changes that happen in recovery, we need help to feel secure. We want the gifts we've been offered, but we can have them only if we keep working and keep growing in trust.

As we continue on the road of recovery, we feel more and more ready. As we come to accept that our program is based on progress, not perfection, we gradually find ourselves spiritually transformed. We are becoming entirely ready.

Today grant me the courage and the
patience to accept the sometimes
slow process of change.

Nothing great was ever achieved
without enthusiasm.
— *Ralph Waldo Emerson*

Many of us can probably recount the details of the "last straw," the turning point, the moment we began the journey on the road to recovery. Up until then all roads, however different, led downhill. For some of us, the descent was steep, rough, and swift; for others, it was long and winding across years of denial, the pain just under the surface.

But today we are on the brink of recovery. Maybe it still looks like the bottom, but now we're looking up. And that's what counts.

Part of looking up involves enthusiasm for life's smaller offerings. We relish the little things we once overlooked: a friendly clerk at the grocery store wishing us a good day; planting seedlings in the spring that, come summer, will yield flowers; the joy of going to sleep with a contented heart.

Enthusiasm breathes hope into our resolve to begin a new sober life. Life looks better in sobriety, and with enthusiasm, it will be better.

Today help me greet my recovery with
gratitude for all that has happened and
enthusiasm for all that can be.

*Everyone has been made for some particular
work, and the desire for that work has been
put in every heart.*

— *Rumi*

All of us are gifted. Every person has a gift that can bring
great joy and light to those who encounter it. Our task is
to stand in the sun and create a climate that will develop
and nurture our gift.

Sometimes we are afraid to let ourselves believe we
have anything special to offer or contribute to the world.
We think of ourselves as plain and untalented, with no
special potential. But if we believe we are limited, we act
in a limited way. We take few risks and follow few paths
that might develop our special talents and gifts.

In recovery, we are learning to love ourselves and trust
ourselves in a whole new way. Now anything is possible.
To fully believe in our talents, we need only step from
the darkness into the sun. We will take this first step,
trust enough, and start believing that, yes, we do have
special gifts.

*Today let me be aware of my deep and
unfilled desires, dreams, and wishes,
which is the first step on the way
to accepting my gifts.*

A faithful friend is the medicine of life.
— The Apocrypha (Ecclesiasticus 6:16)

When a friend loses a job or a loved one, we hurt, too. We wish there were something we could do, something that would ease the pain. It hurts us to see our friends upset and frightened. But our head tells us there's really nothing we can do except stand by and offer support.

We can simply be there when our friends need to talk and listen when silence is best. We can let them know that our relationship is the same, that we don't feel any different about them. We can offer our time, when needed. And we can let them grieve and be angry without criticizing them.

We need to remember that the important thing is our friend's pain, not our own. Sometimes we hurt so badly for others that they end up feeling they must help *us*. In our hurry to stop the pain, we often try to over-control the situation and demand that a friend race through the process of grief. We might try to push our friend into action that isn't right. Now that we can see this pattern, we can try to avoid it. And we can remember that a friend needs respect, not interference. A friend needs love, not pampering or caretaking. A friend needs support, not babying. Sometimes all a friend needs is someone to listen.

Today help me put aside my tendency to "fix" things and simply be there to listen.

Create in me a clean heart, O God;
and renew a right spirit within me.
— Psalm 51:10 (KJV)

Recovery isn't the end of addiction; it's the beginning of a new life. When recovery is new to us, we may focus only on what we've given up—the social life, friends, and lifestyle we once had. We may look back through rose-colored glasses, remembering only the excitement and independence of active addiction. Our new life can seem pretty tame, pretty boring. And we haven't yet replaced our old friends with new ones or our old lifestyle with a new one. So, looking back, we see losses instead of gains. But, bit by bit, we begin to recognize how much better this new life can be for us. We've lost excitement but gained peace and serenity. We thought our choices were free, but now we know we were being controlled by addiction. We thought we had a spiritual life, but now we realize we were spiritually bankrupt. We thought our lifestyle was good, but now we know it was destructive and deadly.

But that's in the past. Once, we were dying a day at a time. Now, we're learning to live a day at a time.

Today help me see my old life as it
really was. Help me be grateful
for the changes I've made.

Some days I feel like a tightrope walker.
— *Jeannette N.*

We all perform a balancing act, trying to keep perspective on what's important and what is not. Sometimes we fall: other drivers cut into our lane, the supermarket line takes forever, the baby starts crying and we lose our cool—and our balance. At those times a minor criticism at work or a harsh word from a friend is just too much.

During our years of active addiction, we were impulsive, living in an all-or-nothing, black-and-white world, completely out of balance. Minor slights became major issues. We were subject to any whim our distorted thoughts cooked up.

We've had lots of practice being out of balance, so we have to work harder to regain it, but now we have the tools to change. Our program gives us a new focus, reminds us of what's important in our lives. We're reminded, too, of our powerlessness over people, places, and things. These ideas are new to us at first. We thought we had to control everything and everyone around us, so we failed. But now we're learning how to keep our balance and recover it when we've lost it. With practice, we'll get better every day. Now, we're learning how to "Let go and let God."

Today help me remember what's important.
Help me keep my balance.

*Recovery for me has been almost a rebirth.
I'm born again as the curious, trusting,
honest child I was so long ago—the child I
thought I'd lost forever.*

— Paul D.

For many of us, that child was just waiting for a chance to find us again. It was waiting only until we could maintain honesty, integrity, and decency. We had to relearn how to live so we wouldn't hurt that child. We had to learn to choose people more carefully so the child's trust wouldn't be betrayed. We had to embark on a new life to protect that child.

Little by little we did change our lives. Little by little that child was reborn. As the child learned to trust us, he or she became more a part of our daily lives. We learned to look to that child for the source of our pain. With the help of our inner child, we're now beginning to heal. In learning to love our child within, we are learning to accept ourselves as lovable, forgivable human beings who are ready to step out into the world and take our place in a loving community of others who are also healing.

*Today help me remember the child within me
and to protect that part of myself
in every action I take.*

Forgive yourself. The supreme act of forgiveness is when you can forgive yourself for all the wounds you've created in your own life. Forgiveness is an act of self-love.
— Don Miguel Ruiz

Our choices in relationships, careers, lifestyle, and self-expression are often influenced by our upbringing. Has the social climate changed significantly since our childhood? Have our family systems changed? Can we find ways to change old, ineffective behaviors?

Recovery offers us the gifts of responsibility and self-forgiveness. Now, as we begin to change, we can let go of the past and its pain. Our ability to change often starts by embracing our inner selves with forgiving, adult arms. In this act, we take responsibility for our own happiness, nurturing ourselves toward the new life we are finding in recovery.

We are earning our own love in a whole new way. We respect and honor our physical selves with rest, exercise, and nutritional food. We stimulate our minds with new ideas and experiences. And we send our spirits soaring through conscious contact with our Higher Power. We feel worthy of love, and we even have enough to give some away. Now we are learning the talent for being happy.

Today grant me the power of self-forgiveness and the gift of hope.

All things pass. . . . Patience attains
all that it strives for.
— *St. Teresa of Ávila*

Some days, it seems like our struggles will never end. The pain, the loss, the heartaches, the failures—we can recount them all. Where is the strength to go on?

What if we began our day by acknowledging that all things pass? That given time, effort, and patience, we can accept or accomplish most anything? But patience does not mean complacency. On the contrary, each day in recovery requires a new attitude, a new outlook that in time generates its own positive energy for growth and change.

We need strength and patience not only in the difficult moments of our new sobriety but also in the easier ones—the days of comfort when things seem to be going almost too well.

Soon, we can look back across the months and see growth. As the skills of the dancer or the carpenter increase with time and patience, so do our skills in recovery. As we grow in recovery, becoming ever more patient, we become ever more in tune with our Higher Power and the promise of a new life.

Today grant me the patience to live in the moment.
Help me be willing to believe that all things pass
and that I can live better in sobriety.

Sobriety is only a bare beginning; it is only the
first gift of the first awakening. If more gifts are
to be received, our awakening has to go on.
— Bill W.

Sobriety is its own reward and then some. Sobriety is a
condition of openness and receptivity to the treasure of
life. It is the ability to view the world through gentler
glasses and hear our fellows with kinder ears. It is the
ability to see things as they really are, instead of how
we'd like them to be. It is a condition of honesty and
willingness to be true to ourselves and others.

On this day we can look out the window when we get
up in the morning. No matter what we see—another
building, a yard, a busy street—it can remind us that
we're not the same people we used to be. We can look
at this world without fear. It won't bite back anymore.

Sobriety is seeing the world with open eyes. It is like
seeing a daffodil as though for the first time. It is the
gift of learning how to view the world as a friendly and
loving place to be. Sobriety is crying without shame and
laughing with abandon. It is a gift that wakes us up with
hope and puts us to sleep with peace.

Today let me cherish my gift of sobriety
and not take it for granted.

See who you are. Own who you are.
Be who you are. Don't apologize.
　　　　　　　　　　　　　—*Jerry K.*

At some point in our recovery, we need to admit to ourselves and others who we really are. Looking inside and pondering our shortcomings is not the most comfortable thing the program has asked us to do. In the past, it's been more comfortable to deny them, to look the other way, to sweep the human-error element under the rug.

But the rewards are great. Once we own our shortcomings, once we tell them out loud to another person, we have taken full responsibility for ourselves—who we are, what we are—and how we have acted.

Now we are closer to our Higher Power, who has accepted us all along. Now we can return to the spiritual support that is always available. When we admit who we are to ourselves and others, we are given the gift of self-acceptance and a sense of belonging to the human race.

By opening ourselves this way, we enrich our relationships with our Higher Power, ourselves, and our fellow humans. These relationships bring a new sense of belonging and meaning to our lives.

Today I will tell myself and at least one
other person who I really am.

If someone is going to control me,
it might as well be me.

— *Sarah B.*

Ours is, and must be, a selfish program. Our recovery must be the most important thing in the world to us. Sometimes friends and loved ones are confused and hurt because we spend so much time and energy working at our recovery. It's hard to explain why—yes, we must go to another meeting; no, we can't skip it just this once.

But however difficult, however hurtful or confusing to others our behavior might seem, we must take care of our own needs first. We're no use to our friends and family if we've relapsed and no use to ourselves, either. Our choices must seem like selfish ones. Our recovery must come first, before the demands of others or even our own comfort. We need to keep our new determination and work toward a new way of life.

In the past, we told ourselves we'd quit tomorrow, that something would happen to make us change. Now, at last, we have the tools to arrest our addiction, but the tools will work only if we use them.

Today help me be in control
of my own destiny.

When I can take care of this body—the house in which I live—with love instead of force, I have a chance at discovering who I am and what I'm made of. I give myself a chance to grow.
— *Jennifer Matesa*

Do we love and care for our body as well as we love and care for our home and car? Do we feel our body deserves full attention and a loving maintenance plan?

Taking our body for granted is easy because of its remarkable durability and regenerative power. We may get lulled into a false sense of "nine lives" body security, believing our physical being will fix itself no matter what.

Self-care takes time and priority planning to be successful. We may find we put off our exercise and nutritional needs, saying, "Tomorrow I'll start taking better care of myself." But sooner or later tomorrow comes, and our body produces symptoms that demand attention.

Learning to love and nurture our body brings rewards without measure. We deserve to reap the benefits starting today.

Today let me realize that respect for my body builds a healing temple in which the rest of my life can grow.

Pray to God, but row to shore.
— *Anonymous*

A sign in an antique store showed a fisherman in a rowboat being tossed about in a storm. The message was clear: the fisherman may have great faith, but now was not the time to put away the oars and kneel in prayer—it was time to pray *and* row!

Sometimes we find ourselves in a storm of trouble, a sea of problems, and we want our Higher Power to get us out. But like the man in the rowboat, the way out is not by prayer alone. The way out is to pray, ask for help, and take action—do something to help ourselves.

Praying, or any other spiritual ritual, won't keep us sober if we don't also commit to our Twelve Step program. Meditating on healing our relationships with others won't help unless we're willing to make amends. Health and recovery are a result of both communication with our Higher Power and a commitment to do our part.

Today help me to pray and take action.

All experience is an arch to build upon.
— *Henry Brooks Adams*

We can learn something from any experience, even one that is painful. In fact, we often learn more from painful experiences than from pleasant ones. When we say or do something foolish or hurtful that causes us embarrassment or guilt, pain gives us a reason to learn and behave differently next time. It may hurt to be arrested for drunk driving, but the pain of that experience may be the beginning of recovery for someone who is addicted.

We can't change the experiences we have, but we can learn from them. Our life is a gift that comes wrapped in what we experience each moment. When we accept this gift and open it willingly, no matter what the wrapping looks like, we put ourselves in a position to discover unexpected treasures. We live life to the fullest, and we learn who we are as we grow. In that way, all experience is positive in building our new lives.

Today let me learn something that will help me grow in wisdom and maturity.

When you forgive, you in no way change the
past—but you sure do change the future.
— *Bernard Meltzer*

Today is full of endless possibilities and dreams. In many
cases, we are limited only by our fear and lack of hope, in
ourselves and others. Each new day we are given a clean
page to live in our book of life.

What freedom we find when we choose to practice the
art of forgiveness! Hanging on to resentment can keep
us trapped in the past and allow our darkest moments to
control our future. Forgiving ourselves and others allows
us to step into this new day as free human beings. Freedom is a gift we give ourselves every time we choose not
to react to a hurtful comment. Holding on to old resentments keeps our creative energy trapped and stifled. Our
choices are these: new freedom or old resentment. We
choose new freedom. It is the gift we give ourselves when
we choose not to let the sun rise on yesterday's script.

Today let me forgive everyone and anything—
past and present—that might distract me
from my spiritual growth.

> *I was so mixed up I tried to be perfect*
> *at avoiding perfectionism!*
> — *Kathryn G.*

Oh, the struggle with perfectionism! Of all the clubs we can use to beat ourselves, that one may be the worst. With all the "musts," "must nots," "shoulds," and "should nots" we demand of ourselves, it's a wonder we can get through some days at all.

One woman said she called one of her cats by the wrong name and then spent the next two hours depressed. Most of us don't go that far with perfectionism, but we still make unreasonable demands of ourselves.

The "one-year" test is a good one for perfectionism: "If I (fill in the blank), what difference will it make in a year?" Some things will be important in a year. Making meetings, contacting our sponsor, communing with our Higher Power, and being honest with ourselves and others are all important. And we should be concerned when we fail. But more often we punish ourselves for the little failures—forgetting someone's name or saying the "wrong thing." These are the "crimes" we remember the most. But now we can learn to forgive ourselves and concentrate on what's really important: our new lives in recovery.

> *Today help me remember what's important.*
> *Help me forgive myself for minor mistakes.*

When one door closes, fortune will
usually open another.
— *Fernando de Rojas*

Sometimes, especially in early recovery, we concentrate on our losses instead of our gains. We see a chapter in our life closing, and we mourn. We must leave some friends behind or say goodbye to a social life we enjoyed. We must give up active addiction, which had become our best friend and only comfort. We may even have to leave our families, at least for a time, in order to concentrate on our own needs.

We need to grieve all these losses. Then we can see more clearly what recovery has brought us. For every loss, we've gained blessings. For every friend gone, we have the chance to make many more. A whole new sober life awaits us when we're ready to be part of it.

When we gave up the false comforts of addiction, we found genuine comfort in sound sleep and healthy bodies, in peaceful days and serene nights. When we were ready to give up anger and resentment, we found generosity and forgiveness toward other people and toward ourselves, too. In recovery, it's true, one door has closed. But another, better, door has finally opened.

Today help me be grateful for my new life.
Help me grieve my losses so I can appreciate
all that awaits me.

It's always something, to know you've done the
most you could. But, don't leave off hoping, or it's
of no use doing anything. Hope, hope, to the last!
— *Charles Dickens*

Coastal redwoods are incredibly resilient trees. A fallen coastal redwood can sprout anew within three weeks. Small trees can endure many years beneath a closed forest canopy without losing their ability to grow rapidly if and when that canopy is opened.

We can be like that, too. No matter how painful our lives may have been, we always have the internal resources to heal and grow into happiness. We now have the strength, insight, and spiritual tools. This combination teaches us that there is no unhappiness too great to be made better. Opening ourselves up to the miracles of recovery, we step from the dark of negativity into the light of possibility and abundance. It doesn't happen all at once, but it does happen—"One day at a time."

Today let me have complete faith
that my unhappiness will be removed
as I work the steps of my program.

Nature is the Art of God.
— *Sir Thomas Browne*

The most relaxing activities may be the ones in which we do absolutely nothing. And if we can do nothing amid the sounds of nature—birds chirping, water burbling in a brook, the wind rustling in the trees—so much the better. During these moments, away from the noise and chaos of our fast-paced, stress-filled lives, we commune most directly with nature and our Higher Power. Without distraction, our bodies can totally relax; there is no danger, no need to be ready to respond to anything. All we have to do is be.

If we live in the city, we can take refuge in its parks, a quiet room, or the library. We can listen to recordings of the sounds of nature. The point is to slow down, to smell and taste the rain, to hear the chirping of crickets and the rustling of leaves and our own thoughts. When we remember nature, we remember—our bodies remember—that we are a part of nature, part of something greater than ourselves.

Today help me hear the sounds of nature
and let them comfort and heal me.

FEBRUARY

Wisely and slow. They stumble that run fast.
— *William Shakespeare*

Recovery is teaching us to think situations through to the end before we act. In the past, we often reacted first and thought later. Unable to wait out the pain, we tried to "fix" our problems by artificial means: alcohol and other drugs, food, sex, excitement. Our only goal was to escape and get relief from the ups and downs of life. Rushing from one situation to another, we seldom slowed down enough to relax and really think through the consequences of our actions.

Now, we're learning to solve problems instead of escaping from them. Learning to sit still with discomfort, knowing it will eventually pass, has given us real personal power in our day-to-day living. What a wonderful freedom to no longer be driven by the demons of obsession and compulsion but instead to experience our feelings as friends instead of enemies. When we allow ourselves to sit with such friends, open to what they can teach us, we will never be alone.

Today let me think difficult situations through to the end before deciding how to act.

*Calmness of mind is one of the beautiful
jewels of wisdom. It is the result of long
and patient effort in self-control.*
— *James Allen*

We can't just flip a switch and turn off our thoughts.
Thoughts of alcohol and other drugs, food, and sex may
still trouble us in recovery. We may even be tempted
into a relapse by telling ourselves, "Well, the thought is
there, so a slip is coming; might as well get it over with."

But in recovery, we do not have to act on every
thought. We must remind ourselves that the thought
and the action are separate. Then we can allow unhealthy
thoughts to pass us by.

We can let go of unhealthy thoughts by talking with
our sponsor, sharing our thoughts at a meeting, reading
Twelve Step literature, praying, or meditating. When
the urge to return to addiction is powerful, we can get
through difficult times by telling ourselves, "This too
shall pass."

Thoughts end. We can choose neither to act on them
nor to judge ourselves for their content. We can see them
as information and then move on, strengthened by our
recovery program.

*Today help me remember that thoughts of
relapse will pass. Give me strength to control
my actions until the thoughts pass.*

Success is not the absence of failure. Success is persistence through failure.

— Aisha Tyler

"I'm such a failure; I might as well drink!" Feelings of failure are powerful excuses to do any number of self-destructive things. The sad part is, most of us set our expectations so high that falling short is virtually guaranteed. Or we're so afraid of taking risks that we never get the chance to find out what would happen if we tried something new.

A forty-five-year-old woman decides to go back to college and halfway through finds she can't continue. She's so busy that she's too tired to go to as many meetings as she'd like. So she drops out of school. Is she a failure? No—she's honest ("I can't do it all"). She's brave ("I tried"). She's sober ("I need my meetings"). And she's smart ("This stress is going to kill me if I don't make some changes").

All we can do in life is try. Be honest and try. No excuses, no blaming, just try. All those so-called failures are notches of courage on our souls. And each notch brings us new peace and wisdom.

Today let me not consider myself a failure if I don't get everything I go after. Help me feel proud to have tried.

In every enterprise consider where
you would come out.
— *Publilius Syrus*

Relapse starts long before we pick up the drink, use the drug, or eat the donut. First we may skip a meeting or two. We might be too busy or forgetful to call our sponsor. One little thing leads to another, like drops in a pail, until we reach the overflow point.

In recovery, we know how dangerous those little things can be, so we need to think our choices through to the end. Missing a meeting may be a symptom of impending relapse. If we're feeling negative toward our sponsor, it's vital that we talk with him or her. Being critical of others, especially people in the program, is dangerous. One of the first signs of relapse, in fact, is refusing to go to meetings because we're angry at one member.

Thinking our feelings and choices through to the end works something like this: "If I don't go to this meeting, it'll be easier to skip the next and the next. Then if I also avoid my sponsor, I can convince myself I'm doing okay even though I'm not. Then if I reject the program, I'll have no support, no reminders about recovery. And without those support systems, I'll probably relapse." To maintain solid recovery, we need to see the parts of our behavior as a whole. Now, we can make healthy choices.

Today help me see all the parts of the puzzle as they
really are. Help me see through my own denial.

Your point of power is always
in the present moment.
— *Louise Hay*

It's taken a lifetime of living to arrive right here, right now. Everything we've done has prepared us for this moment. Yet in this complicated web of life we've spun, threaded through its millions of moments, lay the seeds of our addictions. In looking back, we can see their growth; we can see the lines of stress and tension that run around and through.

Coming to this awareness is critical to our recovery. So, too, is forgiving ourselves for the past. But equally critical to our continued recovery is living in the present, making "One day at a time" more than a slogan. It isn't easy.

It takes a lot of practice to pick ourselves up whenever we fall into thoughts of the past or the future. But doing so is a skill that can be learned, a skill that rewards us with time in all its fullness. To do what we're doing when we're doing it, to be nowhere else but here, now, is to avail ourselves of the power of the present.

Today help me keep my life simple and full
by living life one moment at a time.

All our power . . . lies in both mind and body.
— *Sallust*

Addiction affects every part of our being—physical, spiritual, and emotional. In the early glow of recovery, we often forget the physical part, as though our bodies don't matter as much as the rest of us. But sobriety doesn't end at the neck; our spirit and emotions can't get to meetings without our bodies.

During addiction, we neglected and abused our physical selves. Now that we're in recovery, our bodies need care and repair. A balanced diet is important every day to rebuild bones and nerves and for energy and strength. Exercise strengthens our muscles, improves our endurance, and brings a great feeling of well-being. It also helps relieve stress and tension. And some of us cut back on or eliminate caffeine and nicotine to help soothe jangled nerves and improve our sleep.

All these changes pay big dividends. It's hard for our spirit and emotions to prosper when we neglect our bodies. But with some loving care, we'll feel better, look better, and work a better program.

Today help me remember how important
my body is. Let me give my physical being
the respect and care it deserves.

*In letting go of you, I'm letting you know
that I believe in you.*

— *Sandra Swenson*

Learning to mind our own business is one of life's trickiest lessons. Often, we may find ourselves in the role of "fixer," feeling we are responsible for other people instead of being responsible to them. If we put our foot into the middle of someone else's life, we can get our toes stepped on. We soon discover that most people relish directing their own lives. It's hard at first to step back and let others make their own decisions, especially if we feel we know what's best for them. But letting others tend their own lives frees us to take care of ourselves.

In giving our loved ones back the reins of their lives, we must trust that they know what's best for them and that they'll do the best they can. Our negative comments and critiques are, in fact, just another form of control.

When we live and let others live, we create breathing room. We have more room for ourselves and for others.

*Today let me live my own life and allow
others the right to live theirs.*

> *Owning our story can be hard but*
> *not nearly as difficult as spending*
> *our lives running from it.*
> — Brené Brown

Our egos may struggle with the very idea of being restored. We hate to admit we lost our sanity in the first place. But when we look at the rubble around us, the picture is pretty clear: the way we were living was definitely insane. Our lives lacked order, direction, serenity, and spirituality. We kept trying the same things over and over, expecting different results. This well-known saying is a good definition of *insanity*.

Our egos and our disease blocked acceptance of our problems, but both lost power and control over our lives when we began to accept who we are.

Just as an antique table is restored to its original beauty, we can be restored to sanity. It will take time and effort. There'll be some scraping and rubbing. But, we're worth it. We are valuable creations, and our Higher Power is willing to work with us and restore us. Our job is to do the next right thing, one step at a time.

> *Today restore me to sanity. Bring me*
> *serenity and a sane way to live.*

*There is no greatness where there is not
simplicity, goodness, and truth.*
— Leo Tolstoy

Intimacy is friendship at its deepest level, the profound comfort that comes from complete trust between two human beings. It means being loved unconditionally, as we are, for our spiritual selves rather than as a package with decorative trimmings and marks of status. And it means loving back the same way.

We learn about intimacy from our families of origin. Many of us, however, didn't have very good role models, so intimacy eludes us.

But all is not lost. Working the Steps in a Twelve Step fellowship makes us honest. Then when someone loves us, they love us. We are being who we really are (as best we know) and in so being we can truly open up to another. It doesn't mean we won't get hurt if the feelings aren't mutual, but at least we're spared the effort of trying to be what we're not or living in fear that we'll be found out. On the other hand, if the feelings are mutual, what great joy to finally be with a friend and be who we really are.

*Today help me find the courage to be
as honest as I can be in all that I do.*

The more balanced our lives,
the more serene we feel.
— Ann Smith

Recovery is a balancing act. As we begin to grow and change, we find that balance is a key to opening the door to serenity. In our old using days, we lived on the edge and had become disaster experts. Major areas of our lives seemed to be in constant flux. We had disturbed relationships, little or no spirituality, poor emotional and physical health, and trouble with money.

Today our world is changing. We are coming to value and cherish our serenity and honesty. When one of our major life areas is out of balance, we find that we pay attention. We're beginning to see patterns and, through these patterns, a new hope for real, lasting change. As we move forward, we seem to be losing our high tolerance for confusion and uncertainty. Every new day, our newfound knowledge about ourselves and our spiritual guidance are working together to change our lives.

Today help me find the middle ground and
take the time I need to find my balance.

When you don't know what to do,
get still. The answer will come.
— *Oprah Winfrey*

"Be still," says a mother to her children or a teacher to his or her students. At one time or another all of us have been told to be still, sometimes for good reason.

There is also good reason to tell ourselves to be still. Life is often hectic and stressful. Work, school, family, and social life can pull us in many directions. When we can hardly think because of so many things going on at once, the message "be still" is most helpful.

By stopping what we are doing and being still, we give our body, mind, and spirit a chance to recuperate. We can let the world race on without us. It will still be there when we are done, but by learning the art of being still, we re-enter the world more relaxed. And relaxed, we no longer are reacting to forces out of our control—we are accepting those things and choosing to put our energy into what we can control. Stillness gives us serenity and choices. It is how we work together with our Higher Power.

Today help me practice being still.

A soft answer turneth away wrath:
but grievous words stir up anger.
— *Proverbs 15:1 (KJV)*

There is nothing wrong with anger. Anger tells us we need to pay attention, that something's happening to us. But we may need to learn new ways of expressing anger. We need to take responsibility for our feelings and use "I" statements to tell others how we feel without putting other people on the defensive.

Expressing anger in a healthy way is a skill, and we can learn it. As with all skills, it will take practice to develop new ways of expressing our anger. But we can learn to be assertive, not aggressive, even when we're angry. Our recovery program can teach us ways to let go of anger, and it can help us learn new and healthy ways of telling loved ones how we really feel and what we need.

Anger needs expression. Without expression it builds, it simmers, it stockpiles, it blurts out sideways through sarcasm or whining, and it ferments into resentment. With practice, however, we can make anger an ally instead of an enemy.

Today help me find a healthy way
to express my anger.

*Humility is like your underwear;
it shouldn't show.*

— *Anonymous*

Humility is knowing there are forces outside ourselves, like our Higher Power and family and friends, who have helped shape our lives. There is no humility without gratitude.

It's always nice to be with humble people because no matter how talented or experienced or successful they are, they will treat us with dignity and respect and be genuinely interested in us. Humble people appreciate themselves and other people, and they know the value of others' experiences and wisdom. We know who the humble people are, not because they've told us about their humility but because we can see it in the way they live their lives. In time, we can become more like them.

*Today let me practice humility and in doing so
attain the wisdom and peace it brings.*

*I find beauty in unusual things, like
hanging your head out the window
or sitting on a fire escape.*
— *Scarlett Johansson*

No matter how strong our recovery, we all experience moments of doubt. There are moments when something in our lives seems so bad that we wonder whether our Higher Power has abandoned us or even the world as a whole.

When we notice ourselves doubting the presence of goodness in the world, all we have to do is take a moment to look around us. Whether we are alone in our homes or on a crowded street, we will find things that suggest our fears are unfounded. We may notice a beautiful flower, a newborn baby, a person complimenting another, or a compelling work of art. All of these things, and more, are there to remind us that there are positive forces larger than ourselves at work. And if we can stay sober, a day at a time, we can have faith that these forces are at work within us as well.

Today let me notice all of the good in the world.

*We try to change other people's behaviors
and feelings to feel better inside and to
avoid our own shame.*

—*Darlene Lancer*

We may find it easy to criticize another, to fault that person for what we despise in ourselves. It takes so little effort to take another's inventory. Yet, when we turn the magnifying glass on ourselves, our vision blurs; we're blinded by anxiety. For a long time, substances and harmful behaviors blurred our vision. We were incapable of honesty and perhaps felt no desire to learn or change anything about ourselves.

Now we are asked to get spiritual, to get honest, to look at ourselves, to focus on the changes we need to make, and to leave others to their own keeping.

We can only change ourselves. Recovery asks that we acknowledge our shortcomings and pray for the courage to change the things we can. More than enough self-work lies ahead—enough to preclude our working on others. It's important that we be real, that we not strive to be someone else. This is where the serenity to accept ourselves will come from.

*Today help me tend my own garden
and let others tend theirs.*

What do we live for, if it is not to make life
less difficult for each other?
— *George Eliot*

We are so grateful that we're no longer alone. For years we have hidden within ourselves and were alone with our secrets, shame, and fears. Now others in recovery will be with us, as much or as little as we need or want. We don't have to hide anything from them. Their attitude of acceptance, encouragement, and good humor supports us in ways we have never known. When we allow ourselves the luxury of that support, we are not only meeting our needs, but we are also letting the light of honesty and friendship into our lives.

It feels good not to hide anymore. And now it feels right, more natural. We are coming to accept and love our real selves as never before.

Today help me to be grateful for others' support
and to give support to someone else.

A smile is the shortest distance
between two people.
— *Victor Borge*

Laughter lifts our hearts and opens our spirits to one another. Nothing feels quite as good as laughter when it wells up from deep down inside.

In the past, maybe we distrusted laughter. Maybe it scared us or we thought it superficial. Or maybe laughter was just another mask we wore—we laughed or joked or teased—anything to avoid a situation that asked for seriousness.

Now we know that laughter, like food or sleep, is essential to our well-being. And like any new behavior, it can be learned.

First, we need to notice how we share with others. Are we somber, unyielding, defensive? Or are we open, on the lookout for the best in whomever we may encounter?

We need not remain imprisoned by past attitudes. Just as we now have days when we wake up feeling grateful and glad to be alive, with practice we can channel that gratitude and gladness into our encounters. We have a choice. Happiness and a positive attitude are contagious. The more we smile at the world, the more life seems to smile back.

Today let me be open to smiling and laughing more.
Let me expect good things to come to me.

The space in which we live should be
for the person we are becoming now,
not for the person we were in the past.
— Marie Kondo

Active addiction creates total chaos in our lives. Even in early recovery, when drug use or other addictive behavior has ended, chaos still reigns. Living an ordinary life does not come easily when for years we've lived otherwise. That's the bad news: order doesn't return automatically.

The good news is that order will return and chaos will end with time and effort. One answer to the first question, "Where do I start?" is "First you make your bed." Literally and figuratively, this is a good place to start. We may not straighten out the whole room, let alone the whole house, but at least the habit of making the bed is the beginning of some kind of order. Something is in place. The rest will follow.

We can start small and build. With time, effort, and patience—and the help of our Higher Power, who guides us as we grow in confidence—order will return. We've already seen it starting to happen.

Today help me bring order to my life.
Help me be patient with this process.

It is impossible to feel grateful and
depressed in the same moment.
— *Naomi Williams*

Thank you, thank you, thank you! There never seem to be enough thank-yous to express the gratitude we feel in our hearts.

The miracle of our recovery is a source of continuing appreciation and thankfulness. How lucky we are to have been chosen to receive the gifts of sobriety and abstinence.

We may feel especially grateful to be witnessing the miracles of change in the lives of others who work the Twelve Steps of recovery. What a privilege to watch another person move from despair to hope and serenity. Again and again we see others get better, sober up, and help still others get sober.

We are all part of a healing chain that stretches around the world, from hand to hand and heart to heart. Gratitude is the glue. It wells up inside us and shines out to others as a candle of hope and possibility.

Today let me accept and express gratitude
as the basic fuel of my recovery.

> *The highest possible stage in moral*
> *culture is when we recognize that we*
> *ought to control our thoughts.*
> — *Charles Darwin*

What rules us? Possessions? Passions? Mistakes? Early in recovery, we may have been surprised to discover just how much these things rule us.

Maybe we criticize ourselves mercilessly, unable to forgive ourselves for the smallest error. Maybe we're people pleasers or perfectionists and feel worthless when we fall short of another's expectations or fail to work the perfect program of recovery. Some of us, now financially stable, let ourselves become controlled by things, wanting and acquiring until we find ourselves again on debt's doorstep. Or maybe we've become rigid with self-discipline, unable to loosen up and enjoy life.

The demons of self-doubt, self-criticism, fear, and rigidity all show their faces early in recovery. Struggling with them is part of the process of change. The struggle doesn't mean we're not making progress or that we're slipping back into old ways but that we're facing our problems and taking responsibility for our lives.

We can learn from these struggles. Asking ourselves, "Who owns me today?" can give us the best answer of all: "Just me."

Today help me be my own self.

What we may finally realize, with time,
is that pleasure is not synonymous with
happiness, but rather a temporary grati-
fication of a desire.

— *Victor La Cerva*

One of addiction's most destructive aspects is the binge, whether it be with alcohol or other drugs, food, sex, or gambling.

A lot of times we'll swear it's the last one, but it never is. A day or two or a week or two later, we binge again. This practice may give us temporary bursts of pleasure, but it never makes us truly happy. It satisfies a deep need that willpower alone cannot appease and announces to any who would hear that this is an addiction. If we add up the binges, we can see the disease process. Over years and years and years.

The next time these feelings start, we can call our sponsor, go to a meeting, and talk about how the urge to binge feels. Reaching out enables us to move through feelings without bingeing. It's not an easy thing to talk about, but the relief we get once the urge has passed makes it all worth it. For that we can be grateful.

Today let me use the tools
I've acquired to avoid a binge.

You can never plan the future by the past.
— *Edmund Burke*

Intoxication used to give us something we thought we couldn't get any other way. As addiction set in, the pleasure faded. We kept drinking or using or behaving in ways we knew were harmful because we didn't know how to stop. But as we begin feeling well again and our pain fades, we may forget. The "bad old days" can start to seem like "the good old days," and that's dangerous.

We can learn to block these thoughts and think about something else until the danger passes. It's important to plan for these times, much as we would plan for any other emergency. Maintaining close ties with our sponsor and supportive friends is insurance for rough times. Reminding ourselves each day of the things we can be grateful for in recovery clarifies our thinking. Praying or meditating every day keeps our hearts open to our Higher Power, who can handle the things we can't. And eating well and resting when we need to rest increase our self-respect and ensure that we'll be able to handle the things that are within our control. All these things we can do today, before distorted thinking sets in.

And in doing these things we'll come to believe that the real "good old days" are the ones we're living right now.

*Today help me replace negative thoughts
and actions with positive ones.*

Practice is the best of all instructors.
— *Publilius Syrus*

Rome wasn't built in a day, and recovery doesn't happen overnight. Some newcomers look too far ahead and get discouraged when they realize all the work a sound recovery program requires. But it's really very simple. We learn a few important basics, and then practice, practice, practice. Just like playing the piano or driving a car, we get the essentials first and then practice until we perfect them.

Consistency is important. We don't become abstinent by cutting down on our addiction; it's all or nothing. We can't claim to be honest by lying only on occasion; we're either dishonest or we're honest. We won't learn forgiveness by keeping certain names on our hate list or making amends to just a few. And we can't learn the principles of our Twelve Step program by attending meetings once in a while; we must make a firm commitment to put our program above all other concerns and honor that commitment.

Soon the right thing is our first choice, without much effort and with no pain at all. And one day we realize our practice has paid off in a whole new life.

Today help me practice being the kind of person
I want to be. Help me earn my own respect.

I live in my body, so taking care of it is the
most important housework I can do.
— *Terry S.*

Recovery may mean great strides in mental and spiritual health, but what about our physical health? Often we neglect this aspect of our recovery.

Broadening our recovery to include physical fitness can mean walking outdoors, visits to an aerobics class, or a simple home-exercise routine several days a week. It doesn't have to be the best exercise program in the world, just a simple one that works for us. And it's not something we have to become the best at. Whatever is right for us.

The first step is consulting our physician to find out what's best for us. Then, once we're up and moving, we'll find the benefits of regular exercise to be well worth the effort. When our bodies are fit, we feel better physically, mentally, and spiritually and can fully enjoy all the rewards of recovery.

Today help me exercise.

One of the hardest things to find in life is
fun people. Far too few appear and seem-
ingly fewer survive adulthood.
— *Sr. Karol A. Jackowski*

Fun is something we all deserve to have a lot of. In fact, we can never have enough honest, down-to-earth fun. Nothing brightens our days like a deep belly laugh with a playful friend. What a relief to feel safe and accepted enough to throw our heads back and laugh.

Fun and laughter are life's natural antidotes for stress and worry. Some days we seem to be infected with a dreadful condition called Chronic Seriousness. Chronic Seriousness spreads gloom and depression and paints our days into a black, cheerless corner. How tiring to be faced by this darkness in ourselves and others.

Today, our challenge is to be fun and trust our right to laugh, play, and feel good. Fun and laughter are conta-gious. The more we open ourselves up to good humor, the more we find our family, friends, and coworkers having fun right along with us.

Today let me laugh, play, and be
willing to have a good time.

*I find ecstasy in living—the mere sense
of living is joy enough.*
— Emily Dickinson

Living on the edge of depression and panic, we had little experience with joy. Our hearts were worn and battle-scarred, utterly unfamiliar with the peace that joy can bring.

Days and sometimes years into our recovery, we one day find ourselves sitting side by side with joy. What a new feeling! It's solid; it's peaceful. It has nothing to do with where we're sitting or standing. It has nothing to do with what's going on outside us or with who said what to whom. It is a feeling too happy to be true, and *joy* is the only word that pops into our heads to describe it.

Joy is the gravy of recovery, and it is beyond measure. Now that we are living in a healthy and life-filled way, there's always a chance that joy will find its way into our day. In this knowledge we rejoice.

*Today let me know that joy is the reward of
persistently working my program of recovery.*

When we learn to let things be, they gradually
lose their power; they cease to disturb us.
— *Jack Kornfield*

"Stuck like glue, stuck on you" once could have been the theme song for many of us when it came to our relationships. Fearing abandonment, we latched onto our loved ones for dear life. We were possessive and jealous. Unacquainted with our resources, we had no trust in our ability to be alone. So, when problems arose, we panicked. We cried, pleaded, controlled, schemed, smothered, even terrorized our loved ones for fear they would leave us. Sadly, we found that the more we manipulated and tried to control their behavior, the more they fought back, retreated, and moved away from us.

Caught in a vicious cycle of control, we finally lost all control. Then we began to learn, the hard way, that peace of mind and freedom are found only through letting go and letting others move toward or away from us at their own pace. Most important, we learned that we had much to learn about relationships. From our childhoods, we may have learned little about what it takes to make a healthy relationship.

The first and most loving step in this process is to detach from the problems of others. As we learn to let go, we find a serenity that transforms our lives.

Today let me let go. Help me understand that each
of us needs to work through our own problems.

*It's not true that life is one damn thing after
another—it's one damn thing over and over.*
— *Edna St. Vincent Millay*

In our journey into recovery, it seems as if we keep
traveling the same road over and over. Wasn't that how
our illness began and how it was maintained? That we
kept repeating the same behavior but expected different
results? Although the answer to both these questions is
"yes," we aren't repeating ourselves the same way we used
to. Recovery requires that we travel the same road again
and again but only until we learn what riding down that
road has to teach us.

We still get angry and wonder at life's unfairness. We
still want others to change, get bound up in their suffering, and lose sight of our own. We still feel most of the
same feelings we used to feel and find ourselves in the
same trap again and again.

The difference now is one of degree and duration. Now
we can learn and change our behavior. So when we find
ourselves detoured down that same road again—even
though we think we've learned all we can there—we'll
become aware of it a lot sooner than we used to. And,
unlike the past, we can choose to turn back.

*Today help me be aware of the many detours in my
recovery. Help me recognize the "same damn thing"
when it appears in my path.*

Our disease is cunning, baffling, and powerful.
— *Program saying*

Once on the road to recovery, many of us tend to switch addictions. This is particularly difficult to understand when we have finally achieved sobriety from our drug of choice.

We've worked hard to give up one compulsion only to find ourselves eating more, being drawn to gambling, or seeking out anonymous sexual encounters to fill our needs.

Numbing our inner pain can take many forms. In recovery, we have learned to be vigilant about new compulsive behaviors. Arresting one addiction only to start another is not recovery. Changing our lives is.

Going to meetings, getting a sponsor, communing daily with our Higher Power, sharing with others, and getting professional counseling when needed are all signs of a healthy, focused recovery. When we take care of ourselves, we can avoid switching to another drug. We can truly be sober and free.

Today help me abstain from all substances
and behaviors that can trigger
the addictive process.

MARCH

*Far away there in the sunshine are my highest
aspirations. I cannot reach them: but I can look
up, and see their beauty; believe in them, and try
to follow where they lead.*

— Louisa May Alcott

Sometimes we can feel as if we are surrounded by deep
darkness—confusion, grief, or loneliness can feel like
our most constant companions. But these times can
also become the greatest opportunities for deep healing.
Though we struggle in darkness, it is at this time that
our Higher Power is working the hardest to guide us
through to renewed health and wholeness. It has been
proven time and time again that new possibilities are on
the horizon even as we plow through times of darkest
despair and deepest sadness.

Looking out, inward, and through our pain, we
glimpse that new light of hope. A willingness to believe
there is a light at the end of the tunnel can make even
our most difficult days bearable and filled with growth.
Before they can soar, our spirits must take the small
steps so necessary for change. The glimpses of hope we
occasionally see are those small steps.

*Today give me hope. Let me feel all
my feelings in each small step I take.*

Tolerance and celebration of
individual differences is the
fire that fuels lasting love.
— Tom Hannah

Love is a healer of hearts and a forgiver of pasts. Love waits until we are ready to share and never threatens to leave if we aren't "good enough." Love encourages our growth, wanting us to be all we have in us to be. Love is a resting place and safe haven at the end of a stormy day.

Love protects solitude, and in solitude we find our Higher Power. Love doesn't demand time, words, or promises, but it is delighted at being together and sharing space. Love is kind in all things, especially in honesty. Love freely speaks its mind, not to hurt and control, but to share, inform, and connect.

We can live today by giving this kind of love to each person we encounter. Our reward for this giving is the growth of our own honesty, kindness, and willingness to forgive. And the love we give may return to us.

Today let me trust that love comes
to those who act lovingly.

Yesterday is a cancelled check; tomorrow
is a promissory note; today is the only cash
you have—so spend it wisely.
— *Kay Lyons*

An elderly man said, "I just realized I've spent my life thinking, 'I'll be happy when such-and-such happens.' But such-and-such never happens, or, if it does, I find something new to wait for. Now I realize I've never been happy."

Think of all the todays we let slip by waiting for tomorrow. Other times, we may lose today in dwelling on yesterday. We worry, fret, and fume, thinking of how we could have done things better. We don't know the first thing about tomorrow.

We need to find a reason to smile today. A reason to be grateful for being here today. Today we won't drink, today we are sober, and today we can do or say one small thing that will make us happy.

With the gift of sobriety, today will bring us what we need to be fully alive. Yesterday is gone; tomorrow is a dream. Only today is truly ours for the taking.

Today help me make the most of this day.
Guide me as I work the Steps and
feed my recovery.

*I've finally recognized my body for what it is: a
personality delivery system designed expressly
to carry my character from place to place, now
and in the years to come.*

— Anna Quindlen

The best gift we can give our mind and spirit is to nurture and care for our body. When our body is in healthy harmony, we are able to focus on our deeper needs and gifts. An uncared-for, out-of-tune body can demand all our attention and energy and leave little zest for the rest of living.

Sometimes we take our body for granted, expecting it to keep working well no matter how we feed it or how little fresh air, sleep, and exercise we give it. Sooner or later, that kind of neglect leads to physical problems that can limit our spiritual, mental, and emotional lives.

It's part of our sober work to learn how to love and care for our body so we can develop a daily physical maintenance program that will take us into the healthy years ahead.

Giving our body the respect it deserves will keep it friendly and on our side for life.

*Today let me honestly assess my total physical
condition and make plans to lovingly care
for the temple that is my body.*

*Hope is a renewable option: if you run
out of it at the end of the day, you get to
start over in the morning.*
— *Barbara Kingsolver*

As the architects of our day, we can design and build a
work of art. What a wonderful opportunity to be able to
draw the blueprints of each day. Starting our morning
with breakfast and an air of positive expectancy does
wonders for our emotional outlook.

Learning to look for the good and happy events in
life acts like an emotional vitamin that lifts our feet and
spirits. We are all wonderful works of art, and we deserve
to have days filled with light and good cheer. The more
positive we are, the more we seem to attract positive
people, places, and things into our lives. Nothing is as
contagious as good cheer and a positive attitude. And
nothing can defeat us when we welcome the good things
in life.

*Today help me decide to be happy
and approach every situation with a
hopeful and positive outlook.*

No man is an island, entire of itself;
every man is a piece of the continent,
a part of the main.

— *John Donne*

In active addiction, we were lost and alone. We couldn't trust anything or anyone, especially ourselves. No place was safe for us; no people were safe for us. The loneliness was the worst of it. There was no one to talk with, perhaps no one who wanted to talk with us. Our self-esteem was so fragile we couldn't trust people to be gentle enough, so we simply avoided them. Our spiritual lives were empty, bankrupt.

In recovery, though, all that has changed. Our new-found spirituality has opened a whole universe to us. We've reconnected with ourselves, our Higher Power, other people, and the world itself. Suddenly we belong here, and we're safe here. The world is no longer a lonely and frightening place. Now, it's a loving place filled with people worthy of respect.

As we learn to love ourselves better, we love others better, too. As we earn our own trust, we feel safer trusting the goodness of others. Empowered and enlightened by our recovery, we can recognize people, places, and things dangerous to that recovery. We can forgive them for being as they are, but we can choose to be different. Now, we're connected to the universe, and it's connected to us.

Today help me appreciate my place in the world.

*I'm a very strong believer in listening
and learning from others.*
— Ruth Bader Ginsburg

Ours is a program of sharing, but we can't share what we don't have. No matter how much we talk about serenity, peace, or love, we can't share those things if we don't really have them ourselves. But how do we find them? Humility is a good place to start. Admitting we don't have all the answers and are still struggling can open the door to being helped by those who are further along in their recovery programs. When we keep an open mind and are willing to listen and learn from everyone we meet, we soon discover that everyone has something to teach us. Those still trapped by addiction can teach us how to recognize our errors and how to avoid those pitfalls in the future. When we meet people who radiate peace and serenity, we can notice how they live and try to follow their good example.

We have lessons to learn from everyone we meet, if only we pay attention. We can look and learn and become more the person we want to be. Then we can bring peace and joy to others, too.

*Today help me recognize my limitations
and help me be humble enough
to learn from others.*

*The reality is that change is hard. The good
news is that change is possible.*
— *Michael Graubart*

As we grow in recovery, we look increasingly to our
Higher Power for help and guidance. When we get
around to asking our Higher Power to remove our shortcomings, we have reached a healthy place in recovery by
admitting we actually have some shortcomings.

But there's a difference between asking to be saintlike
and asking to have our shortcomings removed. We're asking for help in changing the things we do that hurt ourselves and others. We are not asking to be made perfect.

When we first come to this challenge, we may discover
we're secretly fond of these shortcomings. The thought of
living without them fills us with anxiety. They are links
to the past and to our family of origin, and it may feel
like betrayal to live without them. All the more reason
to ask for help in removing them; they are danger points
that can prevent sober spiritual growth. But what joy we
find when we ask for help in removing them. Suddenly
we feel we can change, are changing, every day. We no
longer need to flounder out of control, hurting ourselves
or others. Now we can begin to put our lives in order.

*Today help me ask for assistance
and guidance. Help me let go of my
unhealthy links to the past.*

Look inside. See the wonderful and the painful.
Be open to the process of taking an inventory.
— *Margaret M.*

Inventory? We thought we only had to do that when tax time came around. Now we're supposed to look closely at ourselves and write it all down—a pretty scary proposition.

But if we feel the fear and move through it, we'll see and find a lot. To know with whom we're working on this journey through recovery, we'd better interview ourselves pretty well. We have a long way to go together; it will be an easier trip if we start out with an honest look.

But an honest look means giving ourselves credit for all the good in us, too. An inventory isn't just of negatives but of everything in us. We need to be aware of the major roadblock we call "perfection." This has stopped many efforts and is a way of avoiding this self-search.

This is all new behavior for us. It'll feel scary and may be confusing at first. But we can learn to let go of fear and take our time. Now we have support systems and trust in our Higher Power to help us. With the new strength we've found, we can face an inventory with courage and get to know and love our true selves for the first time.

Today I will trust my Higher Power to
guide me through the maze. The reward
at the other end is worth it.

If you listen, you get your own answers.
— *Walter C.*

One of the wonderful things about a Twelve Step recovery program is that each of us gets to decide for ourselves what it means and how it works for us. How often do we stop to think about our place in the big picture? For most of us, it hasn't been an everyday experience. But when the program came into our lives, we were compelled to look at this—and compelled as well to figure out just what shape our Higher Power might take.

It was one of those tasks we needed to do early in recovery. People around us had a lot of different ideas. We talked a lot and listened even more. Finally our own ideas began to emerge. We began finding a relationship with God *as we understood God*. Over time our relationship has changed, and it will continue to change as we journey through life. It's comforting not to travel alone. As we grow in recovery, our ability to accept and understand a Higher Power will also continue to develop. With this growing relationship, we gain courage and serenity every day.

Today I will grow a little closer
to my Higher Power.

Moderation in all things.
— *Terence*

During active addiction, our lives went from one extreme to the other. Depending on our level of intoxication, we believed we were all good or all bad—angels or devils. We abused ourselves terribly, then went on frantic health kicks to make up for it. We made friends—and enemies—in an instant. We quit jobs, left spouses, alienated our loved ones, all on the whim of a moment.

But life doesn't have to be that way. In recovery, we have a chance to learn a moderate, balanced approach to living. With our new healthy mind and body, we can think things through and make decisions based on our long-term good instead of reacting to the feelings of the moment. If we stay up too late one night, we can choose to have an early evening the next. If we're stressed out, we can make time for activities that will help us recuperate. When we've taken on too heavy a load at work, we can find rational ways to rearrange our schedule.

Now we can look to the future and assess our needs based on what we know is good for us. No longer motivated by distorted thinking and impulsive reactions, we can think and plan ahead. Once we took pride in our chaotic lifestyle. Now we can relax and enjoy the serenity of moderation.

Today help me avoid impulsive decisions
and appreciate balance.

What we plant in the soil of contemplation,
we shall reap in the harvest of action.
— *Meister Eckhart*

We all know someone who always has a new plan of action when it comes to his or her life's work but never seems to do anything about it. Maybe we've been this way. In the past, we simply didn't have the tools to make the changes we dreamed about, so we probably didn't get very far. Now, if we are guilty of more talk than action, it helps to remember that all changes, even good ones, are uncomfortable at first. It's easier to talk about looking for work than actually pounding the pavement and facing rejection. It's easier to promise now and act later.

In recovery, though, we're learning how to "walk the walk" and not just "talk the talk." We're learning that reliance on our Higher Power enables us to take reasonable risks. We're learning that making mistakes doesn't mean we are a mistake. And we're learning to trust our thoughts, our feelings, and our instincts. When we are one with ourselves, we cannot go wrong. Our Higher Power won't let us.

Now we can think about things and do them, too.

Today help me act.

Knowledge itself is power.
— *Francis Bacon*

When we were actively addicted, we didn't know what was wrong with us. We tried to control our addiction over and over again, always failing. When we began to recover, we knew we had to surrender, to admit we were powerless, but we didn't know how to go on from there, how to live our lives to maintain sobriety.

The next step was listening to people in our Twelve Step groups tell their stories. They told us their secrets, their successes, their failures. They told us how they were changing their lives. We accepted the help and support of a Higher Power. We were becoming spiritual. We read about addiction and slowly acquired the tools to live without drugs or compulsive behaviors.

As we become more confident in recovery, we test our powers more each day, learning from each effort how to handle situations in the future.

Early in recovery, we knew almost nothing. Over time, we've learned how to change our lives from pain and misery to hope and joy and new growth. For us, knowledge is power indeed.

Today help me be open to new ideas and experiences that can further enrich my life.

Courage is the price that life exacts
for granting peace.
—*Amelia Earhart*

When we feel angry, lonely, worried, or sad, we can ask ourselves, "Is there a pattern here?" That simple question can help us take a giant step forward in recovery. When we feel these things, most of us feel like victims. We're not used to taking responsibility for our part in our problems. If we find ourselves broke again, ending a romantic relationship again, having the same argument this year that we had last year, we may have established a self-destructive pattern. This is not because we're stupid but because we aren't familiar with happiness. So we stir up what we know best: misery.

Looking for patterns in our behavior and accepting responsibility for them takes honesty and courage. But when we put aside our fears and really see what we're doing, we've taken a huge step in changing. Happiness may feel downright strange at first, but we can get used to it.

Today help me see the patterns I create,
and grant me the courage to change.

I told that little five-year-old living inside me how courageous she is and what a great job she did surviving—it was an important turning point in my recovery.

— *Janet P.*

Since addiction and codependency often run in families, it's likely we had some unmet needs as children. Some of us had absent or abusive parents. Some of us grew up in poverty. Others grew up in a place that looked and seemed normal on the outside but was very wrong on the inside.

We can't run from our past or deny what happened. Doing that, we risk repeating the same behavior in our adult relationships. As recovering people, we need to learn how to be our own nurturing parents. We need to love and protect the child who still lives within us. We need to speak to that child with encouragement and acceptance and trust. We're in charge now and can give ourselves what we need to help our spirits blossom and grow. We can't change the past, but now we can change the future.

Today help me replace negative self-talk with words that a kind and loving parent would say to a beloved child.

Embrace and love all of yourself—past, present, and future. Forgive yourself quickly and as often as necessary. Encourage yourself. Tell yourself good things about yourself.

— *Melody Beattie*

When we learn to forgive ourselves, we grow—spiritually and emotionally—in leaps and bounds. As we slowly let go of self-loathing, we begin to breathe with a new sense of energy and purpose. No longer constrained by self-hate, we are able to see the world as friend instead of foe.

We each have a choice about how we view the world. Do we see it as friendly or unfriendly? Do we expect people to be safe or unsafe? Wounded by life, we may find it difficult to forgive ourselves and others. A willingness to forgive ourselves for real and imagined wrongs is like taking a fresh drink of water. Nothing parches and dries out the heart faster than the shame of self-loathing. Nothing refreshes and rejuvenates like self-love.

Living in today, we begin with the simple wish to love ourselves better. Nurturing a friendship with ourselves gives the world a friendlier feel.

*Today let me trust that I am lovable
and worthy of the same forgiveness
I would wish for others.*

*The world is so full of a number
of things, I'm sure we should all
be as happy as kings.*
— *Robert Louis Stevenson*

When we first began recovery, we were sick and lost.
The world seemed a grim and bleak place to us, with no
comfort or relief in sight. We had given up our addiction,
our best friend and worst enemy, and we had nothing to
replace it. We retreated from the misery of our physical
selves, ignoring our bodies and the outside world.

Gradually, in recovery, our vision has cleared and we
can see the world around us again, not through the foggy
eyes of compulsion and need but as it really is, full of
variety, majesty, and beauty. The seasons change. Life
and light shift. Trees, grass, and flowers go from gaudy
to gaunt and back again. The wind changes direction,
announcing rain or snow or sun.

We've rediscovered food, the crackling of wood in a
fireplace, the color of a sunset, the smell of new earth
and rain.

We can be grateful instead of bitter, and open instead
of shut off from others. We are growing instead of dying.
We've found love and warmth. From near-death, we've
found rebirth.

*Today let me take time to look up at the sky
and down at the earth and appreciate
the beauty I see.*

*We have to do with the past only as
we can make it useful to the present
and to the future.*

— Frederick Douglass

Time was, we didn't live in today but only in the past
and the future. We hated ourselves for things we'd done
or said—rewriting conversations in our heads, spinning
endless rationalizations about what had happened. Or
we'd think about the ever-elusive tomorrow. Tomorrow
we'd have a good job, begin recovery, make friends, make
up with our families, have a wonderful place to live, meet
the perfect lover, and begin to enjoy life. Yesterday and
tomorrow took up all our time; there was nothing left
over for today.

Then in our Twelve Step program, we began for the
first time to live in the present. For the first time, we
can savor life and enjoy our surroundings right now. It's
amazing what there is to see when we look around. People
are a delight, too, each of us so alike yet so different.
We see as though through new eyes and notice so much
we overlooked before. Live for today, "One day at a time."
These simple words have the world in them.

*Today help me live for today. Help me
put the past behind me and the future
ahead of me, where they belong.*

If you do not tell the truth about yourself,
you cannot tell it about other people.
— *Virginia Woolf*

Honesty is the foundation of recovery. In active addiction, we lied to everyone, most of all to ourselves. Dishonesty was a way of life for us, as natural as breathing. To recover, we must eliminate it. But first we must learn what it means to be honest. We must eliminate the lies, cover-ups, minimizing, and rationalizations that kept us in active addiction. We must surrender to the truth of what we did and who we were.

Honesty asks that we be alert to the gray areas of dishonesty, the hidden lies. Are we easing up on the serious work of recovery because we're too tired or too busy? We need to examine our behavior and feelings for the real truth: "Am I really too tired, or am I looking for an excuse to relapse? Have I accepted my Higher Power, or am I still trying to do it alone?"

It takes time to understand ourselves, to recognize the everyday dishonesty that can hurt our recovery. But as we learned to be dishonest, we can learn to be honest. Now we have the comfort and support of the fellowship and our Higher Power to help us.

Today help me be honest with myself and others.
Help me recognize my dishonest behavior
even when it's disguised as truth.

*I thought it was a mistake, but I was
afraid to trust my feelings.*
— *Jennie L.*

For a long time, we couldn't trust ourselves in any way. We were good at lying to ourselves and others. We became experts in denial, refusing to consider any opinion but our own. Our choices were based on addiction, not on logic. We were driven by compulsion, not reason. As our addiction progressed, our thinking grew so distorted that we could no longer count on our sanity. How could we trust ourselves when we couldn't even control our addiction?

Then, as we began to recover from addiction, that same mistrust became one of our strongest allies. We hesitated before acting; we questioned ourselves closely to be sure we were doing the right things for the right reasons. Now that we've made progress in recovery, our judgment has improved. We can pay attention to what happened, how we felt, and what the results were. Soon we'll notice that our reaction to dangerous situations is very clear; our gut feelings are accurate. We are trusting ourselves, perhaps for the first time.

*Today help me pay attention to my
feelings and respect my own judgment.
Help me listen to myself.*

Being fearless isn't courage; courage is doing
the right thing even though you are afraid.
— *Jean L.*

Every frightening situation offers us a chance to grow.
Some of us thought that in recovery all roads would be
paved with gold, that all problems would be instantly,
magically solved. We soon discovered, though, that
things weren't that easy; life just doesn't work that way.
But as we met and solved problems, as we conquered our
fears and faced life on its own terms, we learned we're
richer for every challenge that comes our way.

An easy ride can't teach us how to handle a bumpy
road. Strength and character come from experiencing
and overcoming our fears, not running away from them.
Working through our problems teaches us how to deal
with a similar problem next time, how to capitalize on
our strengths, and how to shore up our weaknesses.
Adversity shows us our limits, how much stress and
anger we can handle, how to take care of ourselves, and
how to be truly independent. Now, in frightening situations, we still feel afraid, our hearts pound, our knees
knock, and our hands shake. But we've learned that the
flip side of fear is self-confidence and self-love.

Today grant me the help I need to solve
the problems I might encounter.

Mutual aid is as much a law of
animal life as mutual struggle.
— *Peter Kropotkin*

Admitting we need help can be so hard sometimes, especially if we let our egos get in the way. No matter how huge the problem, we think we have to solve it alone. Yet, how different we feel when someone asks us for help. We find great joy in supporting other people. When someone needs us, we find vast resources of patience and time.

So next time we hesitate to lean on another for support, we can remember how good it feels to help someone else. That can be our gift to others: letting them have the great feeling that comes from giving of oneself to another. We all rely on each other for strength, comfort, and support. So now it's our turn to turn to our Higher Power and to our friends and loved ones. Today we can be human and vulnerable. Today we can admit we need help.

Today let me put my ego aside and ask
for what I need. Let me be gracious
to those who want to help me.

*The only way to get the best of an
argument is to avoid it.*
— *Dale Carnegie*

Nobody wins an argument when our energy is directed toward making someone else wrong. Our feeling of defensiveness is a red flag that can warn us when tempers are getting out of hand. We will meet many people in life who will not see things our way. Believing we are right and trying to prove it to someone else is usually a one-way ticket to hurt and resentment.

There are some people who seem determined to argue. They seem never to have learned the art of listening and negotiation. Deep insecurity and spiritual pain may cause them to become master fighters. Inside, though, they feel so little power that their egos become involved in being right and proving others wrong. If we're like that, we need to work extra hard to restore our self-esteem. If we know people like that, we need to try to be patient. We need to try to understand their pain and tolerate their fears.

Power-based arguments are usually attacking and hurtful. Learning to back down and choose peace is the mark of a solid spiritual recovery program.

*Today let me take a deep breath and
choose peace when I feel my red flag
of defensiveness flying.*

*People who fight fire with fire
usually end up with ashes.*
—*Abigail Van Buren*

How did we get so convinced that our way is usually best? That surely didn't come from a lifetime of constant success. How did we get fixed in our thinking on a given issue? Not from a track record of first exploring all other alternatives.

This rigidity probably helped us survive childhood. But now it's a wall that isolates us. It closes our minds off from ideas that are more in keeping with where we want to be. And it closes us off from people with whom we would like to be.

In recovery, we are noticing others who are not so fixed in their thinking. They don't pass judgment or criticize quickly. Their tranquility is obvious, and we want more of it. Their openness lets them hear more from others, and that is the way to knowledge, change, and growth.

We find that listening to others is now a blessing, not a burden.

*Today help me be open
to the example of others.*

Depression is nourished by a lifetime of
ungrieved and unforgiven hurts.
　　　　　　　　　　　　— *Penelope Sweet*

Carrying old sacks of anger and hurt on our backs often
gives us a gloomy attitude. But many of us had no idea
how much resentment and hurt we were carrying until it
was removed. The sad part is that it takes a lot of energy
and muscle for us to stay tied to someone else through
resentment.

　　The solution is forgiveness, which is an act of courage
that can't be faked. When we forgive someone, we feel
different. We are flooded with a new sense of freedom.
We actually feel lighter and seem to walk taller.

　　Forgiveness begins with an ounce of willingness. For
many of us, the final act of forgiveness is like a miracle.
Out of the seed of our willingness, a flower grows. A
subtle internal shift seems to have occurred in us and
the intensity of the old emotions is replaced with peace
of mind. Resentments were a barrier to this growth;
forgiveness is the beginning of a new freedom.

Today give me the courage to be willing
to let go of old hurts and resentments.

Cast all your cares on God; that anchor holds.
—*Alfred, Lord Tennyson*

To surrender is to win. To fight or run is to lose. When we lose, we are isolated and lonely. When we fight, we can't reach our potential. But when we surrender, we are alive and connected with society.

Surrender does not make us weak. It has helped so many before us reach quality sobriety. What surrender does is make us humble. It forces us to admit to ourselves and to others that we are not perfect. We make mistakes and that's okay. Surrender brings us face to face with the humility we avoided when we were drinking and using. Humility deepens us and improves our character and self-esteem.

Humility is based on a foundation of trust in our Higher Power. We can't let go unless we're sure we won't fall. With the help of our Higher Power, we know we're protected. Now we can fully surrender and cast our cares on a Power greater than ourselves.

Today help me surrender.

That house . . . fell not: for it was
founded upon a rock.
— *Matthew 7:25 (KJV)*

Recovery is like building a house. First we need a solid plan. Next we need the materials. Last we need the labor to build the house.

In recovery, the plan is the Twelve Steps. The materials are literature and time to think and meditate. And the labor is what we get from our sponsor and from our fellowship with other recovering people. We also look to our Higher Power for labor.

When we feel we're at the bottom again and can't take another step forward, sometimes the only difference we can see between now and the old days is that we're not alone. There are probably many other differences. But it's easy to forget them or dismiss them when we're in pain.

Our Higher Power can give us the energy we need to continue building our house when there's a work slowdown. There's a lot of construction, cleaning, and decoration yet to be done, but with our Higher Power overseeing the operation, we can enjoy the process of creation. And we can trust that we'll be there to nail down the last shingle.

Today help me use all the resources
available to me to build my recovery.

To flee vice is the beginning of virtue.
— *Horace*

Some people, places, and things are risky for our recovery. It's tempting, especially at the beginning, to go back and visit, to test our new powers, to brag a little to the friends we had then, showing them (and ourselves) how far we've come and how much we've changed. But we need to remember that those people, places, and things haven't changed—they are just as dangerous today as they were then.

This is a lesson we need to learn again and again. Even after years of sobriety, we're tempted at times to test our new resolve, thinking this time we'll be able to handle temptation. But that's a gamble—like racing a train to a railroad crossing—and for us, the results can be just as deadly. We may not have quite enough time in recovery to resist the allure of old ways and old friends. We may not be strong enough to resist temptation. We may feel vulnerable and worthless and give up the fight to recover. But life doesn't have to be like that today. We can walk past temptation and find the strength to start a new and joyous life—"One day at a time."

Today help me remember the dangers of giving in to temptation. Help me keep myself safe.

*Your friend is one who knows all
about you and still likes you.*
— Elbert Hubbard

No one is perfect, but most of us want to be, especially
in recovery. If we were still able to work or go to school
or do housework when we were drinking or using or
exhibiting compulsive behaviors, imagine what we can
do in recovery. But this kind of thinking sets us up for
failure. Recovery does not mean becoming superhuman.
It means returning to simply being human, with all our
strengths and our weaknesses. It also means accepting
a Power greater than ourselves.

Learning to accept or at least tolerate another's faults
and weaknesses, rather than passing judgment on them,
is crucial to our own recovery and our ability to make
real, lasting friends. First, of course, we must slowly learn
to accept ourselves, stop judging ourselves, and replace
the "bad parent" inside us with the good parent—to
become our own best friend.

As we keep trying to improve in certain areas, we can
learn to love ourselves today even though we are not
perfect and never will be.

*Today help me care enough about me
to be a good friend to myself.*

*Money is not required to buy
one necessity of the soul.*
— *Henry David Thoreau*

Today we live in a society that seems to worship things. Television, movies, and magazines tell us that sophistication, respect, admiration, and self-confidence come from owning things rather than from who we are inside.

Twelve Step meetings are wonderful antidotes for that message. Here is a fellowship of people who don't judge us by our clothing or our credit cards. Here we are cared for because of what's in our hearts, the condition of our values, and our common goal of sobriety. And our Higher Power loves us just as we are.

When we feel caught up in a nonspiritual way of life, we can pause and remember that we have a place to come home to. We can come in from the rat race and rejoice in a fellowship that values honesty, integrity, and spirituality.

*Today help me remember what's
really important in my life.*

Let nothing good or bad upset
the balance of your life.
— *Thomas à Kempis*

The uncontrollable obstacles of life in sobriety are tough enough, yet we often make things worse for ourselves. We may create obstacles of negative self-talk, jealousy, resentment, and fear. These can change our recovery from simple to complex. When we speak harshly to ourselves, we tend to isolate and become passive. When we are jealous, we're not fully accepting ourselves. When we are resentful, we cannot be at peace. Fear can keep us from greater risks and greater rewards.

But we can keep recovery simple and serene. We can talk to ourselves reassuringly. We can become more positive and work on keeping relationships clear of debris. With the help of our Higher Power and Twelve Step program, we can work through our fear and resentment to find lasting peace and serenity.

Today help me keep my recovery simple.
Help me overcome those obstacles
that hurt my spiritual growth.

APRIL

I don't want to stand with the setting sun
And hate myself for the things I've done.
— *Edgar Guest*

We have finally come to terms with many unpleasant things in our lives. The pain of our addiction led us away from who we really were. Now, as we become more firmly entrenched in our Twelve Step program, we learn how important it is to be true to ourselves. We know now that in order to be truly happy, we must be happy with ourselves. At the end of the day if we can look in the mirror and honestly say, "Today I'm happy with me," we are one step further in our recovery.

We can never be so sure of ourselves that there is no room for improvement. When we find ourselves becoming disillusioned and unhappy, we can do an inventory, asking, "Am I the best me I can be?" Maybe our minds need to be stretched and stimulated. Maybe it's time for a modest exercise program. Maybe we need to spend more quiet time with our Higher Power. Doing one small thing can help us feel better about ourselves.

Recovery is a lifelong journey; each day we take another step. When we do the small things to grow, one day, perhaps today, we'll look up and feel the happiness gathering in our lives.

Today let me do the things
I know are right for me.

The mind can't soar if the body's
been grounded for repair.
— Dale E.

When we were young, we could stay up late at night often with no major problems. In active addiction, we could stay out all night and still function the next day, though usually not as well as we could function sober.

Now, though, most of us need a good night's sleep on a regular basis. As we grow and age, we lose the ability to bounce back after little or no sleep. Also, like any other people recovering from a life-threatening illness, we need even more sleep than usual, at least in the early stages of recovery.

Getting a good night's sleep regularly doesn't make us boring people. To the contrary, it makes us alert and well-rested so we can get the most out of the next day.

We honor our bodies when we pay attention to our physical needs. When we are well-rested, we feel better about ourselves. Recovery is a lifelong journey. It doesn't just take place during the day, when we're awake. A good night's sleep, a nap when we're tired during the day, or just a few moments of peace or quiet time taken from a busy schedule are often the best things we can do for ourselves. This is one way we can take healthy control of our lives.

Today let me get the rest that I need.

I never realized something so good
could knock me for a loop.
— *Frederick G.*

We expect to be upset by bad news or at least to be blown off course for a while. But good things take a toll on us too, especially if they mean big changes. We're creatures of habit, and change is hard, even a change to something better. We don't prepare for good things the way we do for bad ones and may not have any support to help us cope. So we sometimes flounder, not sure what to do next. We can take a long time regaining our balance.

Change doesn't have to upset us anymore; we can prepare ourselves. When seeking a promotion or a better job, we can think through how it might affect us. Taking on more responsibility can be scary sometimes. A new relationship, even a new friend, involves more responsibility, too, and more time from us. We need to think about how we'll handle our feelings and get our needs met.

With each change, the most important constants in our lives will be our recovery and the presence of our Higher Power. With the strength and support of our Twelve Step program, we can face change with serenity.

Today help me accept change
and grow from it.

To be powerless is to be empowered.
— *Jerry K.*

"Empowerment"—what a powerful word, what a scary idea! Some days we can't get "out of the driver's seat." We feel frustrated and helpless. Other days we find it easy to admit we're powerless, and we instantly feel ourselves becoming more powerful. We find we can make decisions in our lives. We can do it!

But we can't do it alone. This life of recovery is a "we" proposition. We need to involve other recovering people in our lives. We need to become acquainted with a Higher Power. Together, we will be able to make good decisions and be directed to do the next right thing.

The challenge is to learn we can't change other people, places, or things. But we can play an important role in life's plan if we open ourselves up to the guidance and love of our recovery community and our Higher Power.

*Today I will trust in my Higher Power
and open myself up to the "we" of
my fellow recovering friends.*

Find a group of people who challenge and inspire you, spend a lot of time with them, and it will change your life.

— Amy Poehler

Valuing our friends, we come to value ourselves. Accepting and enjoying the goodness of special people in our lives is an adventure in getting to know the depth of our hearts. Friends teach us about our own capacity to care for and love other human beings.

We stretch our own goodness by listening to a troubled friend when we're tired. We grow when we go out of our way to give our friend a ride when his or her car breaks down. We cherish another and ourselves when we find a card to send on an anniversary. We learn acceptance when we love others in spite of their failings and remind them of their special value when they feel guilty or down.

For many of us, being vulnerable and receiving friendship might be the best gift we can give. It can also be the most difficult. As with other problems in recovery, though, we find patience can be the solution. When we extend our patience and tolerance to others, we find a new inner calm and serenity. And we feel more worthy of love. Learning to be a friend is a two-way street that challenges us to love and to let others love and care for us.

Today let me enjoy the wonder of friendship.

If the only prayer you say in your whole life
is "thank you," that would suffice.
— *Meister Eckhart*

Sincere gratitude is the only attitude that always lifts our spirits. Being grateful for the good things in life can pick us up on days when we seem to be speeding downhill.

Gratitude restores and heals because it lets us stand outside our own small circle of worry to view the bigger picture. It puts us in touch with our Higher Power and the wide-angle view of life. In the light of eternity, how important is our problem of the moment?

Finding something to be grateful for and saying "thank you" gives us hope and a better understanding of our blessings and resources. Some days we may find little to be grateful for, so we start with small things. We start with the ability to get up in the morning and go to bed at night. We continue with flowers, sunsets, the scent of the earth, and so many other things. If we are willing, we will always find an abundance of things to be grateful for.

Today let me cultivate an attitude of
gratitude and hope for my life.

If you are willing to open yourself to the miracles of each day, each day will be a miracle.

—*Katherine L.*

The morning light tiptoes into the room and gently warms us. Slowly, we return from the world of dreams and begin a new day. How can we doubt that there is a Power greater than ourselves? Each day, a multitude of little miracles remind us—if we take the time to notice.

During recovery we learn to wrap our minds around the idea of a Higher Power. It truly is an awakening, a "coming to," after years of fog and blackouts. Our grandiose, self-centered life was like a dream. Then sobriety, an amazing gift, slowly crept into our world. Very much like waking from sleep, we began to open our eyes, see the real world, and open ourselves to the joys and opportunities that awaited.

Now that we have been awakened, we need to keep our eyes open, to listen to the direction and guidance from this Power greater than ourselves. The answers are there if we're willing to stop, look, and listen. We feel these answers every day.

Today help me look at the miracles around me,
especially in Twelve Step meetings.

Peace, peace is what I seek, and public calm;
Endless extinction of unhappy hates.
— Matthew Arnold

Anger is healthy, telling us something's wrong with our world. But hate is anger out of control. When we hate, we can't think clearly. All our attention is focused on the feelings and needs of the moment. The "big picture" is forgotten. All our senses are turned inward to our most primitive feelings and the needs of the moment. We're blind to the pain of others and deaf to the words of others. Our minds can't work well; messages are going out, but none are coming in. Hate is a dangerous state of being for us; we're likely to lash out and say or do things that hurt another person. Some of these things we'll regret later and grieve over. Hate hurts others, and it hurts us too.

In recovery, we can learn to avoid the frustration and feelings of weakness that bring on hate. Prayer and meditation help the most. Contacting our Higher Power can help cool the feelings and bring peace and serenity. With the help of a Power greater than ourselves, hate doesn't have to keep burning in us, endangering everyone close by. We can vent our anger honestly when it is appropriate. We can find calm.

Today help me understand my feelings.
Help me keep anger small and tame
and avoid the fires of hatred.

Seize the day!
— *Horace*

During active addiction, everything was going to happen "tomorrow." We'd give up our addiction, get a good job, make up with our families and friends, call someone for help, go to that meeting, get a new apartment, become honest and decent and proud, learn a new trade, find a better life . . . tomorrow. For today, we'd do the same old things in the same old way.

Now we know today is all we have: the past is over and tomorrow may never come. All we can count on, all we can control, is just one day: today.

But what a world is contained in that one day! We can be abstinent for one day. We can be the best person possible for one day. We can be loving and giving and caring for one day.

In this one day, we can stop to smell the roses and really see the wonders around us. We can give thanks to our Higher Power for the beauty in the world. We can reach out to a newcomer and find support with our sponsor. In this one day, we can be all we ever dreamed we'd be.

Today let me be grateful for all I have,
and let me be the best "me" possible.

The first and worst of all frauds
is to cheat one's self.
— *Philip James Bailey*

Clearly, achieving serenity requires rigorous honesty, especially when it comes to our feelings. We are so adept at masking our vulnerability and imperfections, pretending to know what we can't possibly know, pretending we have no limits. In this way, we often remain untrue to ourselves.

Although it may take many months or even years, we are equal to the difficulty and challenge of rigorous honesty. We can practice openness and avoid using defenses. We can learn to avoid using rage to cover fear and hurt, and we can learn to avoid using smiles to cover sadness and pain.

In recovery, we can learn to know, and tell, our real feelings. We can find harmony with ourselves.

Rigorous honesty can become one of our character traits, particularly when we feel that we no longer have to fear sharing who we really are.

Today help me overcome my fears of being
vulnerable and imperfect. Help me achieve
serenity by honestly sharing my feelings.

Turn it over.
— *Program saying*

"How do you 'Turn it over'?" We often hear this question in meetings. The struggle isn't as much with the "turning over" as with making a decision. When something happens and we feel confused, it generally boils down to one simple question: Are we going to do it our way (again), or are we going to follow the lead of our Higher Power?

Deep down, we know the right thing to do. It may not be easy or familiar, but we need to do it. The start of our problems is resisting change and getting caught up in managing our own lives and the lives of other people. That way, we take a simple task and turn it into a major chore. But if we keep it simple and do the next right thing, we are "Turning it over."

We need to listen to our inner voice. Sometimes it is easy to hear; other times it's difficult because we don't like what it's saying. We need to sit quietly and become peaceful and open. The answer will come. If we can't quiet ourselves, we can go to others in the program and listen to them. They will often tell us what we need to hear.

*Today I pray for the courage to
accept direction and the courage
to follow through with action.*

I always live in the present. The future I can't know. The past I no longer have.
— *Fernando Pessoa*

If we always get what we want, things always go our way, and people always do what we want them to do, we have no need for a Higher Power. Sometimes we have a tendency to think we are all-knowing and all-powerful, and then we are surprised when we are, once again, proven wrong.

It is human to be disappointed when we don't get what we want. But when we dwell on our disappointment, as if we should have gotten what we wanted, then we forget all of the work we have done to learn to let go. Many of us go through the motions of letting go—we may pray to our Higher Power, "Thy will be done"—but still hold on to resentments over the times when things were not done according to *our* will.

We can know only the present moment. This is our life—all of it. When we worry about future wants and past disappointments, we don't leave room in ourselves for the present. When we let our Higher Power take care of the future and live the best we can right now, we can feel assured we'll be ready for the better things that are in store for us.

*Today help me focus on
where I am right now.*

Our greatness has always come from people who expect nothing and take nothing for granted— folks who work hard for what they have then reach back and help others after them.

— *Michelle Obama*

We often read or hear about people who have made major contributions to the well-being of others. Some donate large sums of money to build schools or hospitals. Others perform acts of great heroism or skill in saving others' lives. If only we could do one of these things! If only a great opportunity presented itself so the world could see we really do care.

The problem with waiting for "The Great Opportunity" is that it may never come. And even if it did, the desire to perform great acts often has its roots in a large ego, not a large heart!

If we really want to serve others, there are opportunities every day. Like giving a genuine compliment to someone, offering to take someone to or from a meeting if he or she otherwise can't go, or picking up a dropped object for a stranger.

We don't need to wait for a great opportunity. Serving others in little, everyday ways can bring great joy.

Today may I be willing, in attitude and action,
to reach out and help others.

*Life is a grindstone. But whether it grinds
us down or polishes us up depends on us.*
— L. Thomas Holdcroft

Self-destructive attitudes keep us stuck. Most of us develop destructive attitudes as children; as adults, we don't know how to change. We repeat the same patterns over and over, each time feeling more out of control.

But now, in recovery, we're learning to stop hurting ourselves. We've found people who have "been there" and can help us learn a new way to live. With our Higher Power's help, we can turn over our fears and let go of old anger and depression. We've found a new beginning.

Making this change requires change in body, mind, and spirit. We're beginning to take care of our physical needs, changing our mental attitude, and, with the help of our Higher Power, setting out for spiritual growth. We're replacing self-destructive attitudes with new ones—"One day at a time."

*Today let me graciously ask for help
to change my attitudes. Help me
begin to believe in myself.*

I know all except myself.
— *François Villon*

We've all had friends who give wonderful advice to everyone but themselves, and we all have a little of that in ourselves, too. It's so easy to sit back and see what other people do wrong with their lives. The missteps and mistakes are so clear, the triumphs so obvious to us. Sometimes we give advice; other times we simply observe.

When it comes to our own lives, we're often masters of denial. We can't see what we're doing at all. We bumble along thinking we're doing one thing, only to discover when it's too late that our real behavior has been quite different.

But we're luckier than most people; we have a program of recovery that helps us realize what we're doing before it's too late. With the help of our Twelve Step program, our Higher Power, and our sponsor, we can get a "bird's-eye-view" of where we are, how we're doing, and how we can change to live a better life. With help from our Higher Power, we can risk taking a clear look at ourselves. "One day at a time," we'll come to understand ourselves, our motives, and our behavior better. We may never know ourselves as well as we'd like, but now we can begin the exciting search for self-awareness, honesty, and serenity.

Today help me seek the truth about
myself without fear or denial.

*So teach us to number our days, that we
may apply our hearts unto wisdom.*
— *Psalm 90:12 (KJV)*

Modern technology lets us record the past and predict the future, but the time that is really alive—the time when we're really alive—is now, right this moment.

Up until now we may have tried to block out, distort, or gloss over what was happening. We may be ashamed of the past or fear the future, while we completely miss the real meaning and action of the moment we're in.

Recovery gives us the tools to live in the moment by helping us "Keep it simple," "Put first things first," and practice "Easy does it." We are now more able to see the joy of living this day.

Knowing we are no longer alone, knowing we have the comfort of our Higher Power, each moment gives us the confidence to stay alive in the present in a healthy, sober way—"One day at a time."

*Today help me realize I don't have the events of
yesterday or tomorrow in my grasp right now.
Show me the joy of today.*

If I only see my mistakes, I can't
stay sober very long.
— Ben N.

Many of us review our days each evening just before sleep. This review can be a trial or a delight, depending on the focus. Sometimes we see only mistakes and errors, groaning about what we did wrong and how awful we are. What a self-defeating, depressing thing to do! Looking at only the negatives can discourage us right into relapse. If we're doing so badly, we reason, why continue with recovery?

Instead, we can try concentrating on the good things we did, no matter how small. Did we make someone smile? Did we give a word of hope to a friend? Did we refuse to contribute to a problem? Did we squelch an angry response? Did we forgive an enemy, eat a well-balanced meal, make amends to someone we had harmed in the past, go to a meeting, get a sponsor, tell the truth instead of making an excuse?

As small as they may seem, these are the real indicators of our progress in recovery. They are valid "good deeds" we can be proud of. When we review our day tonight, we can give ourselves the pat on the back we deserve. We've earned it.

Today help me be gentle with myself. Help me
recognize the good things in my life.

I feel like I had a slip today,
and I didn't drink or use.
— *Beth T.*

Aside from a "slip" to drinking or using, we may also have what we call a "behavior slip," a return to an old pattern of unhealthy behavior toward ourselves or others. Behaviors such as lying to someone, losing our temper unnecessarily, or carelessly hurting another's feelings are all too easy to fall into sometimes.

At least now, though, our minds are clear and we can realize it when it happens. We become aware of unhealthy behavior and, thanks to our recovery program, take action. We can make immediate amends and teach ourselves to avoid that behavior in the future.

These behavior slips are not the end of our recovery. They are signs that we are breaking away from old patterns, old ways of living. They are part of the process—painful when they happen but resolvable. And they are happening less and less. We can forgive ourselves for these slips. When they happen, we can share the experience with our Higher Power, group, or sponsor. They can help us heal the wound, make amends, and let go again.

Today help me be aware of my behavior
toward others and honestly make
amends when I need to.

If we can share our story with someone who responds with empathy and understanding, shame can't survive.

— Brené Brown

Guilt can help us. Shame can destroy us. If we feel guilty for stealing, the guilt is speaking to us about our behavior—stealing. But if we feel ashamed of ourselves, the shame speaks to us about our whole person. The more shame we feel, the more we feel we don't deserve quality relationships, jobs, or sobriety. And we'll probably undermine them all, usually without knowing it. Then we feel even more ashamed, and we repeat the cycle.

Recognizing shame when we feel it can help us halt its destructive course. Sharing our feelings with a sponsor or friend can help us feel better. Thinking about when we felt ashamed in the past will help us identify patterns that we repeat because of shame. Shame thrives on secrets. Now we learn to talk about our feelings openly, and we learn we're worth loving.

Today I will know in my heart that I'm not a shameful person. I am worthy of recovery.

If you don't understand yourself you don't understand anyone else.
— *Nikki Giovanni*

Envy comes from a belief that others have more than we have or are worth more. Coming to believe we are lovable lets us trust the healing of our addictions. This process challenges us to take off our masks and get to know our real selves. When we finally have the courage to confront our internal secrets, obsessions, and fears, we are set free. The deep, empty hole in us that cried out for soothing begins to heal, and we feel settled.

The task of accepting our human weaknesses and limitations and loving ourselves in spite of our imperfections is a difficult one, but it is the path of spiritual growth.

Being willing to nourish the healthy seed inside us is one of the first steps that is necessary for the door of recovery to swing open. As we let go of our pain, self-doubt begins to diminish and our real selves begin to flourish.

Today let me trust that there is something
lovable and healthy inside me that is
waiting to flourish.

More things are wrought by prayer
Than this world dreams of.
— Alfred, Lord Tennyson

When we talk with our Higher Power, we admit to ourselves that we need help from a Power greater than ourselves. When we remind ourselves every moment of the day that we cannot live without our Higher Power sustaining us, we will seek an even closer relationship in order to grow and maintain our sobriety.

When we meditate on the word "power," we bring new strength, new energy, and new dedication to our lives. We can draw on this power any time we choose. And we can use our new power through prayer, meditation, and other rituals that connect us to that Power greater than ourselves.

When we devote this time to enhancing our spirituality, we learn to trust and depend on our Higher Power to help us through each day's challenges. We are no longer alone.

Today I will recognize and be grateful for the
presence of my Higher Power in my life.

*He . . . got the better of himself, and that is
the best kind of victory one can wish for.*
— *Miguel de Cervantes*

During active addiction, we were truly our own worst
enemies. No one could have harmed us as much as we
harmed ourselves. We were on a collision course with
death, self-destructive and sometimes suicidal. It seemed
we'd never get the better of ourselves. For most of us, the
pain finally proved to be too much, and we began the
first steps of change.

At first, we desperately held on to any anchor we
could find—"One day at a time"—praying for the help
we needed. Gradually, though, we found we could master
our self-destructive urges. We began to choose people,
places, and things more carefully. We began to appreciate
the world around us in a new way. We learned a new
respect for our body, mind, and spirit. We learned we
very much wanted to stay here and be a healthy, happy
part of the world.

We learned our weaknesses and strengths and how
to be gentle with our fragile selves. Now with the help
of our Higher Power and our Twelve Step programs, we
grow more confident and self-loving every day.

*Today help me continue to grow
in confidence and love.*

No schooling was allowed to interfere
with my education.
— *Grant Allen*

Education doesn't happen only within the four walls of a classroom or school. We can learn in almost every situation, at almost every moment of the day. Our teachers don't need a wall covered with framed degrees from schools or universities. In some cases, our teachers are those who have been through what we are going through. They can light the way for us. Often, they have something we don't—such as serenity—that they are willing to share with us. They may teach us by being an example for us, or they may share with us how they found peace in recovery.

As learners, our main task is to keep an open mind, to be willing to listen, and to ask questions. Most important is our willingness to learn. As the saying goes, the teacher usually appears when the student is ready.

Today may I be willing to listen and learn
from other recovering people. May I also be
willing to teach what I have learned.

*We live in a moment of history where change is
so speeded up that we begin to see the present
only when it is already disappearing.*
— R. D. Laing

Life can be like living in a fishbowl in which we swim
round and round, chasing our own tails. When we
become obsessed with a problem, we may get caught
up in its pain and lose sight of the solution. The more
we worry, the more we seem to fearfully project into the
future. Fear has been described as Future Events Appear
Real. As soon as we step out of today and into tomorrow,
we invite fear to join us.

Living for today is the ability to stand back and be
objective about what we can change and what we can't.
It is our acceptance of our own limitations and powerlessness. It is the wisdom not to bite off chunks of life
too big for us to swallow in one day.

Living for today, we realize that this twenty-four hours,
well-lived, will grow into happier tomorrows.

*Today let me get out of tomorrow's driver's seat.
Let me live in the present.*

Take it easy—but not too easy.
— *Bob B.*

In the early days of recovery, we're so grateful to be alive that we'll do anything, sacrifice anything, to change. Then, bit by bit, we may be tempted to slip back into our old ways. Sometimes we make excuses to skip a meeting, or we lose contact with our sponsor. We need daily reminders of how dangerous this kind of thinking can be. What will we sacrifice in exchange for our recovery? Is recovery worth giving up a social event? Overtime at work? A movie, a play, the ballet, a concert? Spring cleaning? Although recreation is important, we may consider what excuses we have used to avoid the daily work of recovery.

Without our program of recovery, we would have none of these things to sacrifice. When we began recovery, we may have had no home, no friends, no family, no job. Now, we have a life again. Now, we have choices. Now, we have support from people who accept us as we are and who know the struggles we are facing. Now, we have a Higher Power who will be there for us in the worst trouble. Now, this moment, we can choose life over death simply by making a call and sharing our gratitude for a new life or by asking for the help we need. This is all the power we need today.

Today let me remember all that is good
in my life and work to keep it.

Questions are never indiscreet,
answers sometimes are.
— *Oscar Wilde*

Over and over again, we circle the same thoughts in our minds, certain that if we keep chewing on them, we'll be better able to make important decisions. Should we commit ourselves to a new relationship? Is it time to take a new job? Do we need to stand up for a principle?

The harder we try to make that "perfect decision," the tighter and more obsessed we become. It starts to feel like the most important decision of our lives. The very process of decision-making becomes a problem.

Instead of recycling the same thoughts, let us ask, "What's the worst thing that can happen if we choose a given path today?" "Is this decision in sync with ourselves and our recovery?" "Will it work for today?" When we answer these questions, our choices are clear. And when we make positive, healthy decisions, the cycle of worry can stop. Our lives are more serene and more productive.

Today help me to keep my perspective.
No decision is without risk—
but few are irreversible.

He who has a thousand friends
has not a friend to spare.
— Ali ibn-Abi-Talib

When we entered recovery, we had buddies we drank or used with and people we hung out with but often no one we could really call a friend. For a long time, we hadn't been "friend material." Too poor in body, mind, and spirit to be generous, we weren't even a friend to ourselves; how could we be a friend to someone else? Finally, we just gave up on having friends. Our attitude became "Who needs them anyway?"

Then we began to recover and one day realized we had friends. Good friends. Friends worth loving. And the most amazing thing of all: they loved us too. We could have a friend. We could be a friend. No longer unreliable and ungenerous, we could give of ourselves. No longer needing to buy another's love, we can accept love from others. No longer suspicious about other people's motives, we can accept friendship.

In learning to love ourselves and others, we began to accept that other people could love us too. Now we can trust ourselves to be good to our friends. With a growing circle of people to choose from, we can risk being ourselves, knowing that whatever happens, we can handle it. We could not ask for a more valuable gift.

Today help me appreciate my friends
and help me be a good friend to others.

Sometimes I love you and
sometimes I hate you.
— *Kirstin M.*

Even the people we love sometimes get on our nerves. Spouses, siblings, close friends, and other people we care about do not and cannot always meet our needs. Sometimes when we need a sympathetic ear, we get criticism instead. Other times we may want to be held, but we get a cold shoulder. Love may change to hate, only to change back again to love at another time. Add addiction to this love-hate relationship and our moods may swing out of control.

In recovery, we may set ourselves up for disappointment if we believe the love-hate swing will end forever and only love will remain. We are not always going to get warm, loving feelings from those we love. Even in recovery, those we care about continue to be human with their own needs and concerns.

Our feelings will change, too. But when feelings of anger or hate surface, we need not despair. Our Higher Power is always with us. By working our program, we learn to talk about bad times, learn they will pass, and come to believe that love and acceptance will surface again. Now, we can begin to recognize the pattern of real life and accept changes in others and ourselves with serenity.

Today let me accept the realities of love.

*We're so kind to other people. Why are we
so mean to ourselves?*

—*Allen A.*

Loving others more than ourselves is common in recovery, especially at the beginning. We quickly learn to accept and love others, even with all their flaws, but we use another set of rules for ourselves. Maybe it's because we know our own secrets. Maybe our self-esteem still needs an overhaul. Perhaps we think others are guilt-free. Whatever the reason, we can't really love others until we love ourselves; we can't give away something we don't have.

Luckily, we're learning new ways to boost our self-esteem. Some of us spend a few minutes before sleep reviewing the day, with special emphasis on the positive things we did. Some of us give ourselves positive strokes through the day, telling ourselves what a great job we did or how much progress we've made. Others pause each day for a "quiet time" or meditation. Still others make up a list of tasks and try to perform one each day. There are many other ways to feel good about ourselves, too; all we need is a little creative thought and effort. But it's worth the work. We're valuable, worthy of love, and gaining the tools to learn to love others.

*Today help me be kind to myself
and forgive my faults.*

By speaking of our misfortunes
we often relieve them.
— *Pierre Corneille*

In addiction, we were isolated and alone, ashamed to share our thoughts and feelings with other people for fear of rejection. We lived with denial and dishonesty. With no close friends to mirror our lives, we had no objective view of how we were doing.

Now, in recovery, we can feel overwhelmed by what lies ahead, by all the changes we need to make. Alone, it may seem too much for us. We're still struggling with addiction, "One day at a time." We've begun the work of recovery, but we may feel we're of too little value to ask another person for help.

Overcoming those feelings with the help of friends, a sponsor, and our Higher Power can bring a new strength and comfort to our recovery. In asking for help, we feel better about ourselves. When we get the help we need, we're more confident about trying again. A sponsor can enrich our recovery, giving us that objective view we need so badly and offering the personal affection and spiritual support we've missed so much. With all this love, we are not alone anymore. Help is here when we need it.

Today please help me ask for help and accept
the help I receive with grace.

MAY

Defeat is not the worst of failures.
Not to have tried is the true failure.
— *George Edward Woodberry*

Any new task, especially an important or difficult one, can cause anxiety. We can think of all sorts of reasons for not beginning a task, but the real reason is often fear of failure. We don't want to look foolish or have people laugh at us or look down on us because we didn't do well.

The irony is that just the opposite is true. Most people admire someone who has tackled a major task, like learning a new language, going back to school, or getting into an exercise program. Trying new things takes a certain amount of courage, and most people respect those who at least try.

Getting sober, arresting an addiction, is probably one of the most difficult tasks anyone can do. Sometimes, as we are working on recovery and wondering how on earth we can gain and maintain our program, we forget we are not alone. It's normal to have a certain amount of doubt and anxiety, but that is not a reason to quit trying. We can be assured that the doubt and anxiety fades as, in time, we come to accept our powerlessness and the help of our Higher Power. With our Higher Power near us, we are not alone.

Today help me take a risk and
not be afraid of failure.

*It was the turtle who won
the race, you know.*
— *Jessica S.*

In early recovery, we can get so excited about change
that we want to change everything in our lives, often
radically, and we want to do it right now.

That impulse can be self-defeating. It took a long time,
sometimes years, to progress in addiction; it will take
time to make progress in recovery, too. We need to look
for small, slow changes rather than big, dramatic ones.
And if we look closely, we can already see results.

Are we sleeping better? Feeling physically stronger?
Have we gotten medical care, if we needed it? Has our
nervous system settled down? Are we feeling less jangled, more calm? Are we able to concentrate better?
Have we lessened our fear and anxiety? Do we feel more
at home in the world? Have we found a Higher Power to
share our lives? Do we feel a kinship with other people?
Do we feel more serene in our relationships?

If the answer to any of these is "yes," we've already
made measurable progress in our recovery. The rest will
come with time. As the tortoise showed us, slow and
steady wins the race.

*Today help me to rejoice in small victories.
Let me be satisfied with small successes.*

Ah, what is more blessed than
to put cares away.

— *Catullus*

There's nothing like a good hearty laugh to pick up a gloomy day. Laughter has such a calming effect on us; doctors ought to prescribe it: "Take two jokes, and call me in the morning." Laughter liberates the tormented soul and soothes the troubled heart. Laughter helps us keep perspective; our troubles are less scary, our woes are dimmer, life is less frightening.

No two of us laugh at the same thing; our sense of humor is as unique as our fingerprints. It doesn't matter what we laugh at—our favorite movie, our own silly mistakes, or the circus clown falling on a banana peel—we're always richer just for doing it.

Laughter works on our bodies like stationary exercise, banishing tension and bad thoughts as it loosens the muscles and soothes the mind. A good laugh leaves a happy glow that helps us fend off the ghouls and goblins and things that go bump in the night. Laughter is song, it's joy, and it's life itself.

Today help me bring the gift of laughter
to another person, and help me find
more laughter in my own life.

*The spiritual life does not remove us from
the world but leads us deeper into it.*
— Henri Nouwen

There is a story about a wise woman listening to the woes of a friend. The friend sadly reported her problems on the road to recovery and how stuck she usually felt. After an hour of listening to negativity, the wise woman said, "Remember, God hasn't quit his job."

When we tackle all of life's problems by ourselves, we quickly tire and get frustrated. We can usually measure our level of trust in our Higher Power by our physical and emotional condition. The more trouble we try to carry and fix ourselves, the more exhausted and frustrated we feel.

It is difficult to admit we need help to carry our load. But when we finally let go and turn over a problem to our Higher Power, the clouds seem to open and the sun of hope shines on us again. And though it's not something we learn to do all at once, in time we can see our slow and steady progress and feel our growing serenity and confidence.

*Today I will trust my Higher Power enough to
share my burden. I will turn one thing over.*

You should go to a pear tree
for pears, not to an elm.
— Publilius Syrus

Before, our social life probably revolved around people and places where alcohol and other drugs were available. Now, some days can be full of conflict until we find a new life where temptation isn't a problem. It does no good to waste time wishing we could be with old friends and enjoy that old excitement. We gave in to temptation many times before, and the results were always the same.

No matter how serene we feel, chances are a time will come when we're just too discouraged, too depressed, or too disgusted to fight the urge to have "just one more" binge. We may recover from that relapse—but we may not. So for us, there is only one choice.

Once we make that choice, a whole new world is waiting for us, with things we never dreamed we could be part of. Every city in the country has free or low-cost places to visit, things to do. Old hobbies and interests we gave up years ago seem interesting again. People are waiting out there for us, too. Once we thought everybody was living in chaos just like us. Now we know the world is full of sober people just waiting for us to join them.

Today help me look for the good things in life.
Help me stay open to new possibilities.

*If they dare not forgive, what
becomes of harmony?*
— Fyodor Dostoevsky

We may think we're being noble when we refuse to forgive ourselves for things we did in the past, but this
false humility is often another form of denial. If we truly
accept that addiction is a disease we did not ask for, then
we are willing to forgive ourselves. If we still think it's a
matter of willpower and strength of character, then of
course we won't forgive ourselves for not being strong
enough or smart enough. And if we don't think well
enough of ourselves to forgive, how will we treat others?

Accepting our human limitations is a major step
in recovery. Now we don't expect ourselves to be all-
powerful. We've surrendered to powerlessness and come
to believe our Higher Power will help us. We don't have
to do it all alone, and we don't have to be perfect. Now
we can accept, forgive, and love ourselves with our faults.
We can find harmony.

*Today I recognize I have a disease.
Help me accept my powerlessness.*

How long does it take before
you want to go to meetings?
— *A newcomer*

Often, we don't feel like a meeting. After working all day, we're tired, and going to a meeting sometimes seems like too much trouble. We have to force our feet to move. But we go, and every single time, something magical happens. We feel loved, we feel we belong, we feel that the world is a wonderful place and we're part of it.

Other people talk, telling us their hardest secrets. We may talk and tell them our secrets, and our burden lifts; we're free again. We're part of the love that fills the room, sharing our struggle and serenity with others as they share theirs with us. We are not alone, and we can be grateful for all the reminders we have of this. Whenever we need to listen or talk, whenever we need to feel accepted or loved, whenever we need to share our joy, there is a meeting waiting for us. Now we have the choice of life or death, and we can keep that freedom to choose by choosing life.

Today let me choose life even if
I'm tired or afraid.

A wise man is strong; yea, a man of
knowledge increaseth strength.
    — Proverbs 24:5 (KJV)

Relapse so often seems to begin with overestimating our strengths and underestimating our weaknesses. The seeds of relapse are planted long before the actual event. Addiction is too strong for us; we must work hard to arrest it. If recovery is to become a lifetime experience, it's our job to learn our limits and avoid things that can frighten, tempt, or bully us into relapse. We can start by learning to recognize areas that are dangerous for us. We can ask ourselves, how solid is our Twelve Step program? Are we going to meetings or avoiding them? Have we chosen a sponsor? Are we following the recommended Steps of recovery?

During active addiction, we couldn't make sane choices. But, now, every day, we're getting healthy again, and we can avoid relapse. Asking for help from our Higher Power and Twelve Step group will give us the support and the answers we need. As we grow in recovery, we learn how to build on our strengths, not our weaknesses. We are changing and finding love, "One day at a time."

Today help me see my behavior clearly
and recognize when I'm in danger.

Dare to reach out your hand into the darkness,
to pull another hand into the light.
> — *Norman B. Rice*

Some days, we may be too shy to reach out to other people. We're not alone. Others may be shy, too. Often, we can get the help we need by offering it to another. When we can overcome our shyness enough to offer support to someone else, we feel better about ourselves and the world. Soon, we'll find it easier to reach out to other people, to begin a conversation or ask for help ourselves. Those efforts succeed far more often than they fail. We don't have to let shyness keep us from others.

We discover that giving blesses the giver as much as the receiver. Our Higher Power always sees to it that we get what we need. All we need is to be open to that strength.

Today help me reach out to others
and share of myself.

Where there is patience and humility,
there is neither anger nor vexation.
— *St. Francis of Assisi*

When we begin recovery, we often start tapping our feet and looking at our watches, impatient and annoyed because our family and loved ones haven't embraced recovery from their own unhealthy behaviors. But if we really care about them, we'll give them the respect they deserve and let them choose their own recovery timetable, as we chose ours.

We began recovery when we were ready and not a minute sooner. We may have resisted the urging of others for a long time before we actually felt ready to change our lives.

Now it's our turn to give others the time they need to change, to let them recover on their own timetable. We're tempted to rush them, and we may be overeager to share the joys of recovery, our new values. We've found a wonderful new way to live, and we can't wait for them to join us. But wait we must. Our Higher Power can help us wait lovingly and with patience, and we can let go.

Today help me be patient with those
who are new to the path of recovery.

Real love is like holding an egg in your hand.
The tighter you squeeze, the more you lose.
— Ron P.

When we learn to love the beauty and gifts of others as separate from us, healthy relationships can flourish. Control is the enemy of love, and at the heart of our painful relationships is usually one person trying to change another.

When we let it, love grows into a flower of unsurpassed beauty. When we trust enough to allow our loved ones to really be themselves and make their own decisions, we open the door to intimacy. Nothing is more loving than feeling free to live without criticism from our partner.

Learning to love someone better challenges us. It isn't easy, and we run up against our deepest fears of rejection, inadequacy, and loss of control. But these are things we don't want to bring to a relationship anyway.

The work we do to improve our own health is the most important task in our lives. Part of this work is to let others do the same for themselves. When we can begin to do this, we are beginning to be ready to reap the rewards of real love.

Today help me let go of others,
especially those I love.

I can know my Higher Power
through daily meditation.
— Lucille S.

When we are at a Twelve Step meeting, our Higher Power is there also. One way to experience that Power is through members sharing their strength and hope. We know our Higher Power is working in our lives when we hear others tell their story, and we don't have to feel alone again.

We can ask ourselves, are we trying to find ways to identify with other members, or are we still trying to be different? Are we finding fault with our Twelve Step program, or are we grateful for the principles we are learning? Do we criticize or judge others at meetings? Or are we at one with our Higher Power and the force of our fellowship?

We can, in recovery, strive continuously to improve ourselves. We can let go of the criticizing and faultfinding we did in the past and live day by day, grateful for our sobriety. By doing this, we are living constructively, growing spiritually, and freeing ourselves from pain. We are open to the presence of our Higher Power, who is always within and who can help us if we only ask.

Today I will seek to feel my Higher Power's
presence and power in my life.

Holding on to anger, resentment, and hurt only gives you tense muscles, a headache, and a sore jaw from clenching your teeth. . . . Forgiveness gives you back your laughter and the lightness in your life.

— Joan Lunden

Our past addictive lives were often based on denying our feelings. Some old habits die hard, and unresolved anger may creep back into the best of recovery programs. Unexplained bursts of anger may take us by surprise and make us wonder if we really are getting better. Finding ourselves faced with a string of daily irritations, we are now challenged to really look at our hearts and minds.

What might we be ignoring and covering up in our day-to-day living? Discovering the cause of passive-aggressive anger is a powerful tool that will let us live assertively with our feelings and then let go of them. We don't have to let our feelings build. With help from our Higher Power and our Twelve Step program, we can work through the real cause of a problem.

It's always better for us, and others, if we share our feelings rather than store them up till they burst out. In learning to do the next right thing, we learn to be assertive with our anger, and we find real peace of mind.

Today let me learn to assertively share my feelings instead of covering them up.

Why pick thorns, when you can pick roses?
— Karin W.

We've all known unhappy souls who seem to spend their whole lives collecting insults, searching for proof that the world is a terrible place. "What did he mean by that?" they wonder suspiciously. Expecting the worst, that's usually just what they find.

Bad things happen, but something positive can be found in almost every situation. Sometimes it takes close looking, but it's there if we're willing to apply faith, time, and hard work.

Life is like a jigsaw puzzle; we see only one little piece at a time. Who knows what wondrous things may come from today's misfortune? Mold growing in a messy lab turned out to be penicillin. Clothes that no longer fit us and clutter our homes can be treasures for those with fewer resources. And the same rain that ruins our outdoor plans grows our food. Unhappiness, misery, insult, death, and destruction come to us all. But so do goodness, beauty, decency, love, and comfort. We find what we look for.

Today help me be patient with bad news
and annoyance. Help me pick the roses
instead of the thorns.

Iron rusts from disuse; stagnant water loses its
purity and in cold weather becomes frozen; even
so does inaction sap the vigor of the mind.
— *Leonardo da Vinci*

Being idle is so easy that sometimes we want to make it a full-time job. Our lives are filled with getting to and from places, with work, with family and friends, with obligations and requirements and rules to remember. When we have spare time, we're tempted to just sit back and take it easy. But this can be habit-forming, and soon the easy way is the only way we're willing to go. It's too cold to go to a meeting. It's too much work to call our sponsor. We've put in a full day; now it's time to relax and take it easy. The television comes on. It's too much trouble to read, to think, to change.

This attitude is dangerous for us. In recovery, there's no standing still. We either go forward or we go backward.

When we become more active, we soon discover we feel stronger and more alive. We are more excited about life, happier, and more fulfilled. We look forward to spending time at peace with our Higher Power. There is so much to know, so much to see, so much to do in the world, and every minute of every day is our chance to be part of it. In time, we find ourselves looking forward to doing all we can do and becoming all we can become.

Today help me take advantage
of all that life offers me.

Anger is a momentary madness, so control
your passion or it will control you.

— *Horace*

When we're angry, our minds and bodies are completely involved. Our blood is pumping, our pulses race, our breathing is fast and furious, and our brains are on temporary hold. We are no longer rational beings. We become anger machines, ready to put up our fists and fly off the handle on a second's notice.

In recovery, we want to be different, and learning to deal with anger is a good place to start. We've learned we can't afford to be impulsive—that's what got us into trouble before, and it'll do it again if we let it.

How do we deal with anger? We can turn our anger over to our Higher Power, and we can pray or meditate to find peace. Or we can try a rational approach, working to understand the other person's point of view. We can honestly vent our anger. Or we can simply retreat, backing away until the anger subsides and we can think more clearly. All these methods give us a chance to catch our breath.

Now we don't have to act on every feeling or react to everything that happens. We can choose how we'll handle our anger. And if our choice turns out to be inappropriate, we can learn from that as well.

Today let me treat my anger as a tool
for growth, not as an enemy.

*One of the quiet pleasures of old age
is that we can more comfortably be
who we really are.*

— *Karen Casey*

Growing old is not something most people look forward to, and unfortunately prejudice against older people seems to be common in our society. Beautiful young adults have often been used as models of the ideal human form. Older people are left out entirely, or they are shown as clumsy, slow, and unable to think or act with grace and dignity.

Yet, when we study history and current events, many of the leaders in the political, business, and artistic communities are older. There is wisdom and experience in age that can be gained no other way, as well as a perspective on life most younger people don't know about.

We don't need to deny our aging process. We don't need to lie or joke about our age. Respect of self and others who are older is a sign of spiritual maturity.

We may not be able to do all the things we could when we were younger, but with age comes growing wisdom, perspective, and serenity that can be a blessing if only we look for it and appreciate it in ourselves and others.

*Today help me give thanks for the blessings of age
and appreciate those whose years are many.*

· MAY 18 ·

> *We're all under the same sky and walk the
> same earth; we're alive together during the
> same moment.*
>
> — *Maxine Hong Kingston*

It's easy to keep wanting more and to forget to give
thanks for the blessings we already have. The world is
such a beautiful place. We can spend eternity taking it
all in, appreciating the wonder all around us.

Sometimes, we get caught up in our petty affairs or
become so absorbed in our day-to-day lives that we forget
to observe. At those times, we may notice only what we
don't have, rather than giving thanks for what we have.

When that happens, it's time to stop and look around.
Comfort and beauty surround us, if only we take a
moment to appreciate them. Our Higher Power has
given us a universe of opportunity, free for the asking.
We are in recovery. We have the dazzle of sunrise and
sunset, the complex workings of our own bodies, friends
who care, and a program to follow for a new life.

It may be a struggle, and we may be tempted to give
up, but part of recovery is taking time to notice what we
have. Life is filled with so much to be thankful for, if only
we can learn to look for it.

> *Today help me see beyond everyday matters
> and realize the richness of my life. Help me to see
> what I have, rather than what I don't have
> or what I think I should have.*

Fear knocked at the door. Faith answered.
No one was there.

— Unknown

Fear invades so much of our lives, spreading like a blanket of heavy fog. Fear wears many masks: doubt, procrastination, alarm, timidity, shock, terror. Fear has knocked on our door and we have let it in.

To be human and accept our limitations is to accept that we cannot make it without help. When we accept our humanness, we learn we are truly deserving of the help available from our Higher Power. Recovery has brought us faith—faith that our Higher Power will show us a new way to live, with confidence in ourselves and our friends in recovery. Faith lights the way and burns off the blanket of fog that once shrouded our lives.

Faith is our weapon against fear, as fear slowly leaves our lives.

Today may I be open to the power
of faith and live in the light.

In many ways, fear is the force that stands
between human beings and their dreams.
— *Barack Obama*

How many times have we read or heard stories of people who achieved greatness despite all sorts of obstacles? We may think there was something about their genetic makeup that enabled them to do more than the rest of us. That is not the case.

People who achieve their goals despite many obstacles are not superhuman. What they may possess, at times, is an intense, clear focus on the goal they wish to achieve. It's like walking across a beam suspended above the ground. If you focus on the goal—the platform at the end of the beam—you are likely to walk across. But, if you take your eyes off the goal and look elsewhere, say, at the ground below, you will probably think about falling and not reach the goal.

Sobriety and abstinence are the goals for us. We may wonder if we can achieve these goals because of the obstacles we face. But we have help from our Higher Power and Twelve Step program. If we focus on our goals each morning and remember those goals throughout the day and in the evening, we can avoid the obstacles we face and find success and joy in our new lives.

Today help me to keep my goals of sobriety
and abstinence in constant sight.

How poor are they that have not patience!
What wound did ever heal but by degrees?
— *William Shakespeare*

Do we often begin the day worrying about all that has to be done? Even feeling unable to act because there's too much to do? When this happens, we are usually taking on too much. We are loading down the present with worry about the future and trying to do everything at once. We are forgetting about patience.

We have only one moment to live, and that moment is now. We cannot sustain life by taking tomorrow's breath today, and we can't make ourselves happy in this moment by trying to settle the next day's problems.

When we take on too much, we can ask for help. This skill is a new freedom in our recovery. It's a way of accepting our limitations. Taking a single action toward our goal, we are doing what we can today, and we can let go of tomorrow. We can be calm, patient, and more serene. No worry over the future is worth sacrificing today's serenity. Today's serenity and today's careful action will bring us just what we need tomorrow.

The rewards are a newfound patience with ourselves, the help of others who care, and a new life of peace and tolerance.

Today let me slow down and do what
needs to be done each moment.

Sometimes I feel sorry for people who
don't have a Twelve Step program to
help them solve life's problems.
— *Eleanor L.*

Recovery helps us handle many issues that beset and befuddle other people. Whenever we hear someone say, "I'm a grateful alcoholic," we know what that person means. We're grateful, too. Before our addiction, lots of things bothered us. Since we started our recovery, though, we've learned that everybody has problems, no matter who they are or what they do. The difference is that now we have the tools and the support to help us get through.

So much of life is spent muddling through little difficulties, but we're lucky enough to have a recovery program and Higher Power to help us handle just about anything. Now there is always a place we can go to share our thoughts, hopes, and feelings. Our problems haven't disappeared, and we don't expect them to. But now we have the tools and support we need to work through our problems each day.

Today I am grateful for the tools
my Higher Power has given me.

*The manner of giving is worth
more than the gift.*
    — *Pierre Corneille*

Most of us grew up learning it's better to give than to receive. While it is true that it's good to give to others in need and to think of others before ourselves, some of us become dependent on giving as the only way we can feel good about ourselves. Our self-worth is so low that giving becomes necessary to our self-esteem and we are blind to what others are trying to share with us.

Now, we're learning to share our blessings with others and let others share with us. We may share our feelings and thoughts, our time and talents, and our money and possessions, especially with those in need. But we need to be gracious and willing to receive what others want to share with us, too. The fellowship of our Twelve Step recovery program is based on such a willingness to share. Giving and receiving are meant to exist together, in balance.

*Today may I be willing to receive
what others wish to give me, even as
I am willing to give to others.*

Joy is a return to the deep harmony of body,
mind, and spirit that was yours at birth and
that can be yours again.

— *Deepak Chopra*

There are three key aspects of our recovery: body, mind, and spirit.

We know that taking care of our bodies is essential to recovery. That means eating properly, exercising as much as we can, and not abusing ourselves physically.

Taking care of our minds is also important. We are trying to make choices that enhance our recovery, not diminish it. This includes the things we read, watch, and listen to. We seek out education and positive affirmation. We go to meetings. We gather with others who share our vision.

Spirituality is the common thread through all of this, for without it we are lost. Our spiritual search is our effort to improve our conscious contact with a Power greater than ourselves. Through this search comes harmony of body, mind, and spirit.

Today let me care for all three aspects
of my recovery: body, mind, and spirit.

Language alone protects us from the
scariness of things with no names.
— *Toni Morrison*

Sometimes, we may feel as if we have created a "false self." Often, after we've been in recovery for a while, we begin to realize that we've been wearing a mask and hiding behind it. We did it to protect ourselves from the pain and uncertainty of our lives. And during those years of drinking or drugging or bingeing, we had no interest in learning who we really were.

Have we created false selves to mask our real personalities? As we grow in recovery, our reclaimed honesty will help us answer this. When we're true to ourselves and our feelings, we'll come to know and enjoy our values. We are becoming people we respect and love. We'll come to make better choices, building a new life around our real selves.

We can establish our true selves by sharing openly our thoughts, feelings, needs, desires, and concerns with those around us.

Today help me share who I really am.

Everything's got a moral,
if only you can find it.
— *Lewis Carroll*

We must make many choices in our recovery. Some of these will strengthen our character, for they will be hard to make and sometimes even harder to accept. One of the most meaningful sayings in our program is "Let go and let God." We understand its true meaning when we are faced with adversity and we feel needlessly hurt.

If we are to let go of a problem, we must feel in our hearts that no matter what the outcome, our Higher Power has a special purpose for us. We may not be able to see that purpose now, but if we let our Higher Power guide us, we will be guided down the right path. If we do our best to detach from our pain and try to see a more peaceful future, we will feel more secure. Given this security, we'll be free to direct our energy toward positive, healthy choices that will bring us more of the happiness we deserve.

Today help me "Let go and let God,"
even when it hurts.

You have been criticizing yourself for years, and it hasn't worked. Try approving of yourself and see what happens.

— Louise Hay

Why is it some days when we wake up and look in the mirror, we feel saddened by the view? We have been our own harshest critics. The sound of that inner voice scolding us can be deafening. It can drown out the real music in our lives. We would never greet a friend this way; why do we treat ourselves so harshly?

There is a good, loving human being standing in our shoes and all the power of a loving Higher Power waiting to be recognized. All we need to do is be quiet, look a little longer, harder, and more gently, and we'll see and hear our Higher Power.

Our way of life is changing and improving each day, at our own best pace. With gentle patience, we begin to become more aware of our Higher Power. As we do, we will be able to listen and be guided by this loving, calming voice within.

Today may I speak and listen to myself with respect and joy.

No mention shall be made of coral, or of pearls:
for the price of wisdom is above rubies.
　　　　　　　　　　　　　　　— Job 28:18 (KJV)

We've all been to meetings where we pick up a nugget of wisdom that helps a great deal. It's often something we've heard before but never thought of in quite that way. A nugget could come from someone whose story we've heard hundreds of times or from a newcomer. There's no telling.

It can be especially helpful to keep these nuggets in a special part of a journal. Take the slogans "One day at a time," "Keep it simple," and "Easy does it." These offer particular insights that we keep coming back to. We can collect others and add them to that list. We can go back over the list when we need to or when we're asked for some help. It feels especially good to pass them on at other meetings we may attend. Each time we do this we remind ourselves of their wisdom, and we often find a new insight into our own recovery. These slogans, and our Higher Power, can help us keep changing and learning.

Today let me be open to learning
and hearing things in a way I hadn't
thought of before.

How important is it?
— Program saying

The young man in the meeting was very angry and upset. His lawn mower had broken down. He was having a cookout in his backyard that evening, the yard looked terrible, and he'd paid a lot of money for that mower! After he went on for some time, an older woman gently interrupted him and asked, "Was anyone hurt? Was there danger? Would your guests walk out?" And, finally, "Did you lose your sobriety over it?" The young man smiled, as he answered "no" to all the questions. "No, it was not that important after all."

We all overreact sometimes to situations, people, and events that, later, we see were really not important. The next time we are bothered by someone or something that threatens to ruin our day, we will try to remember to ask ourselves, "How important is it?" If it's not important, we'll spend our time and energy on what is important. There is a world of difference.

Today help me to know what is important,
to forget what's not, and to ask others
for perspective when I'm not sure.

Your self-worth is determined by you.
You don't have to depend on someone
telling you who you are.

— *Beyoncé*

As children, we often played at what we wanted to be when we grew up. As adults, when we try to be something or someone we're not, there isn't the same opportunity to play-act and return to our "old" self as we did when we were children.

As adults, we find that our recovery progresses when we begin to be content with who we are. This means accepting our flaws as well as our strengths. It may also mean letting go of some dreams we had as children and accepting the fact that it's okay not to be the company president or the basketball star. It doesn't mean we've failed if we aren't perfect or haven't become superstars. Happiness and serenity come from loving ourselves as we are, rather than wishing we were someone else.

Today help me recognize that I don't need
to be anything, or everything, I'm not.

Love truth, but pardon error.
— *Voltaire*

Often, we don't like to admit it when we are wrong, even though simple logic tells us no one can be right all the time. And much of what we often argue about as right or wrong has nothing to do with right and wrong. Is it right or wrong to wear a red dress rather than a blue one? Or to take the bus rather than the train to work?

Life is too short to always try to be right or to put everything into the category of right or wrong. We save ourselves a lot of grief and pain when we are able to admit we made a mistake and avoid using the labels "right" and "wrong" when they just don't apply to the situation. We find great freedom in letting most things just be what they are, without a judgment from us. And we learn to love ourselves and those around us the same way.

*Today help me to admit when I am wrong
and not gloat when I am right. May I not
see everything in terms of right or wrong.
May I avoid being self-righteous.*

JUNE

If you feel distant from your
Higher Power, who moved?
— *Program saying*

We're often amazed by the wonders of nature. It's hard to feel significant when we think of the vastness of the universe. We may wonder how a Higher Power can care about each of us with all the planets, stars, and conditions of the world happening at once.

Then we realize we're putting our own human limitations on our Higher Power. This is also a clever way our ego promotes us to the status of a Higher Power.

We need to "Let go and let God." We need to remember that our significance is no more or less than anyone else. It's not easy to put trust in someone or something other than ourselves. But when we do, we begin to recognize that everything unfolds as it should.

Today I will keep things in perspective.
It will be refreshing to let my
Higher Power manage the world.

Two halves do not make a whole
when it comes to a healthy relation-
ship; it takes two wholes.
— *Patricia Fry*

Active addiction made our lives a series of jealous, angry
rages followed by passionate appeals for forgiveness.
We may even have grown to embrace pain like a lover,
stroking our ever-present guilt. This was our life when
it was empty of love. Our capacity for love, to give and
receive, became misguided. Our drug of choice insisted
on sole devotion and repaid us with despair.

Sober love offers and requires appreciation and understanding; it allows us to step back a little and watch
another's growth; it gives us hope both within and
beyond ourselves. Sober love is not so much a feeling as
a series of loving acts, chosen freely. It is not ownership
of another but support for another's freedom.

Today let me free myself and others
to love without fear.

We can offer support, encouragement,
and love, but we cannot live another
person's life, only our own.
— *Beverly Conyers*

Just as addiction affects the whole family, so does recovery. The principles we learn often improve many aspects of family life: we are more open, more calm, more honest, more eager to share, and more ready to listen.

But some family members may be resistant to recovery in any form. We have found the best way to respond is by detaching with love. We must protect our own recovery and not try to change others.

Families can be a source of strength. If we do our own part and learn to detach with love, we give others a chance to see firsthand the joys of recovery. Detachment with love is a beautiful tool when others choose not to support our recovery. We can keep growing and avoid getting tangled up in the resentments of others.

Today help me remember that what is true
for me might not be true for someone else.
Help me practice recovery principles
in all my affairs.

*All you have is that hope that, as you go
through your daily routine, by the end of
the day you will be a little better in all
respects, and do something meaningful.*
— *Mikhail Baryshnikov*

How we choose to start a day will set the tone for the
rest of the day. Will we make time to take care of all our
needs today? It's important to eat a healthy breakfast and
exercise a little each day. Our bodies feel refreshed by a
hot shower or a comforting soak in the bath. Our bodies
need rest. Sometimes we need a good night's sleep, other
times just a nap. In this way, we care for and nurture our
physical selves. Are we also tuned to our spiritual needs?
Do we make time to stop and visit with our Higher Power
on a daily basis? Too often, we ignore our spiritual needs
and our souls go hungry. A daily meeting with our Higher
Power is as important to our spiritual health and growth
as a meal is to our bodies.

This spiritual time we set aside each day offers our
souls the opportunity to quench the thirst and satisfy
the hunger for spiritual food and drink.

*Today let me care for all my needs. Help me
to respect my body as well as my soul.*

If you don't like something, change it. If you can't change it, change your attitude.
— *Maya Angelou*

We are the makers of our daily attitude, and we are responsible for the light or gloom we put on each morning. What a wonderful gift we bring to ourselves and others when we choose to wear a happy smile and look at the bright side of life. This doesn't mean we should neglect our sorrow and losses, for we can share those with our group, our sponsor, or our Higher Power. It does mean we have a choice each morning as we decide whether the world feels basically friendly or unfriendly.

Greeting the day by expecting the best in people and events helps us create an atmosphere of joy and goodwill wherever we go. It is our program in action.

Today let me believe the world is basically friendly and trust that good things will come to me.

No one should let yesterday use up too much
of today. Easy to say, hard to live.
— *Andrea Hairston*

We have so many memories, and it's sadly true that often the unhappy ones are easiest to recall. Sometimes these memories dog us through a day, and the past tinges our present with sadness. This keeps us from being at our best, but it doesn't have to happen.

In our recovery, we are learning to live each day and to relish the present moment. This means not letting old hurts, guilt, and shame from the past invade our lives today. What has happened is done. What is to happen will take place in its own time, at its own pace. In this day, at this moment, we are alive, and we are free to choose how to feel and what to do right now. We are free to feel grateful for the chance to live again. We are free to take advantage of this chance to do our best. If we need help, we are free to ask for that as well.

By living in the present the best way we can, we are also ensuring that good memories will be our gift to our future. Each day that we live as well as we can makes our lives more worthwhile, more content, more our own.

Today let me enjoy the moments I am in,
for they are all I have.

I love being able to say, "I was wrong"
or "I made a mistake" and not feel like
it's the end of the world.

— *Carol C.*

Before recovery, we felt so guilt-ridden we couldn't bear to admit we were less than perfect. Since our insides seemed so awful, we clung to an outside appearance of perfection. That way, we hoped people wouldn't find out what we were really like. But we fooled no one, not even ourselves, for very long.

In recovery, we have a chance to change that pattern. Now, we can learn to admit our limitations, our mistakes, and our imperfections. What a wonderful relief not to have to be perfect. We can be just who we are—very human beings who are groping toward the light. Sometimes we find it, sometimes we lose our way, but still we strive onward. And, in the process, we find serenity and ourselves.

Today help me keep working toward
perfection, but let me forgive my
mistakes along the way.

So much has been given me I have no time
to ponder over that which has been denied.
— Helen Keller

The young man was heartbroken. His fiancée had called off the wedding and left him for another man. "How could God let this happen?" he asked. The young man was convinced God did not care about him. Years later, as he celebrated his tenth wedding anniversary, he told his wife he was grateful to God for their marriage. Now he knew that when his first fiancée left him, it was for the good. At the time, he just could not see it.

We all have moments in life when we lose something—a partner, a job, or something else that seems very important at the time—and feel our Higher Power has deserted us. Sometimes we may feel that having an addiction is a sign our Higher Power has deserted us. It may take a long time in recovery, but we eventually realize that life now is even better than it was before our addiction set in. We appreciate our loved ones and ourselves more than ever, our priorities have changed, and we have a relationship with a Higher Power that didn't exist before. And every new day, we gain a new perspective and insight into how our Higher Power is working to enrich our lives.

Today I will remember that my
Higher Power is always with me.

Wisdom is the reward you get for a lifetime of
listening when you'd have preferred to talk.
— Doug Larson

A good salesperson is usually a good listener. Being a good listener also helps in being a good parent or spouse, neighbor or friend. When we are truly able to hear what others are trying to say, we are better able to enter their world and let them into ours.

Listening to the collective wisdom of others helps us gain understanding and perspective on the world around us. When it comes to recovery from a life-threatening illness like addiction, listening to others who are in recovery is like receiving a gift of ideas.

It is not always easy to listen, because it's often our nature to want to be the center of attention. But listening is an art worth developing. It enriches our lives, improves our relationships, and helps us feel better about ourselves.

Today may I enrich my spiritual life
by listening to others.

I'm finally learning how to take care of myself.
— *George P.*

Giving to others is perhaps the most gratifying feeling of all. We get so much more back from others—thanks, self-esteem, that warm glow we all love. So why don't we thank ourselves that way? Are we ungrateful for the loving gifts we bring to ourselves? Is someone else's opinion of us more important than our own?

We can turn that around, learn to give and accept self-gifts as graciously as we give to others. We can begin by offering some praise for the good things we do for ourselves. Good nutrition can be a boring grind, or it can be something we give to ourselves to strengthen our bodies. Tasks to complete can fill us with dread, or we can think ahead to how good we'll feel afterward to have accomplished so much.

When we're willing to admit we're worthy of love, we begin to be able to do these small things for ourselves. We begin to recognize how loving we are, and we bring that joyous new love to others, too.

Today help me to give and accept love freely.

Afoot and light-hearted I take to the open road,
Healthy, free, the world before me,
The long brown path before me leading
wherever I choose.

— *Walt Whitman*

Being able to make free, healthy choices is a great gift and one that requires careful thought. The greatest choice we have made is our desire to live a sober life. It was a difficult one but one that will lead us to other healthy choices. "One day at a time," we choose what is important in our lives and what is not. We learn to make healthy decisions—those decisions that promote our recovery and a peaceful life.

It helps to remember that we are human; just because we are sober doesn't mean we will always make the right choice. Working our program gives us all the tools we need to make choices for who we are and what we are to become. But if we fall back into our old behavior and make some bad decisions, we will learn from those, too. Growth comes not only with success but also with failure. Now, our mistakes can help us grow and become stronger every day.

Today let me choose from my heart
what is best for my recovery.

Loneliness is caused by an alienation from life.
It is a loneliness from your real self.
— Maxwell Maltz

There is a vast difference between being alone and being lonely. To be alone but in touch with ourselves can be very rewarding. But to many of us, the isolation and alienation we feel in our loneliness are devastating. To feel that we have no one, not even ourselves to depend on, can lead to despair.

Belonging to a group that shares our pain and has lived through our experiences will help end our isolation from ourselves. A Twelve Step group validates our feelings, shares our grief, helps us learn to love and trust our Higher Power, and shares our hope for the future. A group can also be the source for a sponsor, someone we can always go to. Instead of feeling different, as we have for so long, in our group we have a place to feel a part of others and to accept ourselves.

Continuing to be a part of this fellowship, we learn how to accept who we are, and we learn that being alone with our true self can be a creative and joyful process in recovery.

Today help me be grateful for all those who
so freely give of their love and support.

> *I realized that if my thoughts immediately affect my body, I should be careful about what I think. Now if I get angry, I ask myself why I feel that way. If I can find the source of my anger, I can turn that negative energy into something positive.*
>
> — *Yoko Ono*

Anger is a way we regain our sense of self-respect and entitlement. We realize now that nothing is worth feeling like a doormat. We naturally feel angry when attacked, but we may lack the skills we need to appropriately channel our feelings. Sometimes confrontation is necessary; other times we are best served by turning things over to our Higher Power. Whatever we need when we are angry, sober living equips us with the tools to identify and share our angry feelings and to find new options to help us maintain our dignity.

Now we can be thankful for our newfound ability to see more clearly what our anger is about and how we can deal with it. Now we can use and appreciate this healthy internal "alarm system" to grow and change. And we can turn our anger over and let go of lingering resentments on a daily basis.

*Today let me share my anger honestly
and then let go of it.*

Humility is the surest sign of strength.
— *Thomas Merton*

A life lived in recovery stands in sharp contrast to a life of active addiction. Before, we knew only pain, fear, and confusion. At times, death seemed better than life. But in recovery, we're reborn. Suddenly all is possible, and life is blooming. There is not only hope; there are daily results.

Only a tremendous force, a Higher Power, could bring such a sweeping change to our lives. We stand in awe of the changes brought by recovery. We are humbled by the grace we've been given to lead a new life. If we follow the Steps of our Twelve Step program, we will have the strength to find a new, sober life, "One day at a time."

*Today I am humbled when I think of
the strength the program offers.*

*I've been working two programs from the
beginning. That's what works for me.*
— Bert T.

Today, more and more of us are working more than one
program. In some cases, a problem with food surfaces
after we gain sobriety from alcohol or other drugs. Or
it could be work addiction, sex addiction, gambling, or
addiction to excitement. Often, we need to work an
Al-Anon program along with an Alcoholics Anonymous,
Narcotics Anonymous, Cocaine Anonymous, or Over-
eaters Anonymous program.

Those of us who work several programs know the
benefits and great healing power that can be unleashed.
Sometimes we find the programs working together. We
find a common ground. Other times, we find different
programs addressing different needs. All our programs,
though, stress communion with our spirituality and a
Higher Power.

We are grateful today for the vast number of Twelve
Step programs that help us heal our addiction or addictions. And we are grateful to find the people we need,
as well as the opportunity to share our own experience,
strength, and hope.

*Today I am grateful for the variety of help that is available
and for the understanding that working more than one
program is a sign of strength and quality of recovery,
rather than weakness or shame.*

Consider the little mouse, how sagacious
an animal it is, which never entrusts its
life to one hole only.

— *Plautus*

Active addiction left us unable to create an even flow of events. Even now, when we strike a balance, we feel old urges to engage in unhealthy, irresponsible living. Over time these urges fade, but it's still a dangerous time for many. We unwittingly seek to re-create the old familiar life because it's comfortable and seems most natural to us. To guard against this, we need to maintain our desire for steady, serene recovery.

If we can punctuate our days with a manageable routine, we will enjoy greater stability. We can begin the day with a quiet time for prayer or meditation; include healthy meal plans; set time aside for exercise, work, school, or family; and stay in contact with others who share our recovery. The routines of good rest, exercise, regular meal times, prayer, and meetings are the skeleton on which the body of our recovery program can grow. Each of these activities is a reward in itself and serves to remind us of what our new lives have to offer.

Today help me enjoy my regular schedule
of activities as gifts to myself.

We like someone because.
We love someone although.
— *Henri de Montherlant*

In recovery, we are learning that the people in our group love us "in spite of" what we often think of ourselves. Before, we may never have felt we could be liked for who we really were. We were always changing to fit what we thought other people wanted. We tried to please others. We put on "false selves." We hid behind what we thought others wanted. We ended up unhappy and made others unhappy in the process. Now we understand that people in our group may not like every aspect of our character, but they like us. Our sharing of these experiences becomes a strong, common bond.

We all have defects we must work on, and there is no better place to do it than in the fellowship of caring friends who understand the pain and suffering that come with the territory. And the care and generosity of our Higher Power and our sponsor help us love and forgive ourselves. God's hand is on our shoulder, ready to lead us down the road to a more peaceful life.

Today let me do one special thing
out of respect for myself.

It is such a great moment of liberation when you learn to forgive yourself, let the burden go, and walk out into a new path of promise and possibility. Self-compassion is a wonderful gift to give yourself.

— *John O'Donohue*

The Twelve Steps offer us a whole new spiritual attitude. They teach us how to develop a relationship with our Higher Power and how to identify specific obstacles in our path. Working the Steps moves us toward self-forgiveness. We take a look at ourselves and the past, and we air all the shame, grief, and pain by admitting to our Higher Power, to ourselves, and to another human being the exact nature of our wrongs. In this way, we break our painful isolation.

Admitting our wrongs to another human being is perhaps the most difficult but in the end the most liberating act. When someone else truly forgives us, we can begin to forgive ourselves. Through this process, we can begin to feel closer to our sponsor and to others around us, whether at work, home, or in our recovery program.

Today help me find forgiveness in my heart for myself as well as for others.

I still have bad days. But I don't panic when I do.
— *Dan B.*

For many of us, having a bad day is part of the process of getting better. A bad day doesn't necessarily mean a slip or a return to drinking or using. It could mean being secretive, snapping at someone, being rude or grandiose, or feeling those "old feelings" again. We know what bad days are. And we will probably always have bad days. They're part of life.

They are, however, not a sign that we are bad people or that we aren't getting better. We are. For the most part, our lives are much better than they used to be. And an occasional bad day or series of bad days is often part of the healing process. We may even come to view a bad day as a challenge. By responding to the challenge, by choosing a healthy action or clearing up our anger before it turns to resentment, by turning more quickly to our sponsor and our Higher Power, we are growing. Bad days offer us something that good days don't—the challenge to grow, to be honest, to turn things over—the chance to pick up and use the tools recovery has given us.

Today help me to remember that "bad days"
aren't the end of my recovery. They're part of
everyone's life—recovering or not.

Recovery is a journey, not a destination.
— *Program saying*

There is no single point we reach when we are "recovered," when everything is all done and "in order." It's not that easy, nor should it be. Recovery is a process, a way of living that supports and revitalizes us physically, mentally, and spiritually. Recovery becomes the sum total of all our efforts and experiences. It signifies our efforts to change. It is driven by spirituality.

We're not ill one day and recovered the next. No one book or concept will do it. It's not an intellectual place or level of understanding. And it's not affected by our age or depth of experience.

Recovery is something that is a part of us every day. We live it. Even during hard times, we know the process of change is happening. It gets better and easier, but it's never really over. It's a new life, and it's one we're thankful for.

Today help me remember that recovery
is a journey, not a destination.

This above all—to thine own self be true.
— William Shakespeare

Being true to ourselves means more than not imitating others. To be ourselves, we need a sense of self. Recovery involves taking a look at what's inside. We can learn who we are and who we would like to be. We can begin to change a little at a time, earning our own respect.

Being true to ourselves also means making decisions based on what is best for us in the long view, not simply what can be attained right now or what is easiest.

Recovery calls us to be honest with ourselves and motivated by personal integrity in our relationships with others. As we learn who we really are, we find it easier to live with honor. As we make progress in recovery, we recapture our pride and self-respect.

Recovery is a time of self-discovery and, through sharing ourselves with others, our sponsor, and our Higher Power, we slowly learn more about who we are. Now, we can be true to ourselves.

Today may the mirror of recovery help me
see myself more clearly, and may I be true
to the personal vision I see.

Happy Monday.
—*Anonymous*

Most of us, even if we have to work weekends, are thankful when it's Friday. We look forward to the break in our routine, to sleeping late or going out in the evening. Our schedules tend to be different on weekends; there's time to relax, time to worship in a formal setting if we choose.

So how can anyone say, "Happy Monday"? It depends on how we view our work. If our work is meaningless or boring, it's difficult, to say the least, to return to it, but in time our recovery can help us find work we enjoy. And for many of us, work is an essential part of life. It helps us feel we belong to something greater than ourselves and that we are contributing to the health of that greater something, which in turn contributes to society at large. And we're compensated with a salary, satisfaction, or both.

Every day, even Monday, is a gift, given to us without charge and offering us a chance to create happiness.

Today help me be grateful
for every day I am given.

If we don't change, we don't grow.
If we don't grow, we are not really
living.

— *Gail Sheehy*

Our acceptance of life grows steadily in recovery. Faith and trust, two natural foundations of sobriety, help us nurture a healthy flexibility. If we consider recovery as a weaving, we can imagine the strands of hope, joy, serenity, willingness, and surrender intertwined to form flexible strength. It helps, in times when we need to bend with the tide, to acknowledge the inner power of this fabric. With the help of our Higher Power, we can travel smoothly through transitions and weather the stress of disappointment, rejection, loss, frustration, anger, shame, and remorse.

Life, of course, will go on being itself, and we will always face obstacles. But our old rigidity in facing life's obstacles will no longer cripple or paralyze us. We are learning balance and finding serenity. We are learning to accept, to detach, and, through our Higher Power, to have faith.

Today let me gain more balance by learning
to stand firm as well as to yield.

I am alone with the beating of my heart.
— Lui Chi

Addiction and codependency rob us of our natural connection to others. Isolation is the consequence and symptom of these illnesses.

Recovery restores and continues to nurture the skills so critical to healthy relationships: honesty, openness, and detachment. It is essential to our recovery that we can be intimate with ourselves and enjoy our own company. Solitude offers us the chance to relax, meditate, pray, dream, invest in hobbies, and be with our Higher Power. We are replenished from time shared in this way.

When we are good company alone, we will be good company with others. And, with a Power greater than ourselves active in our lives, we are never really alone. Just as our bodies need sleep, our minds and hearts need regular solitude to be fully expressive, attentive, and loving. We, and our friends, deserve nothing less than the richness life has to offer.

Today help me make room in my life
to comfortably sit alone.

Ask, and ye shall receive.
— *John 16:24 (KJV)*

Somewhere in our past life, we may have picked up the idea that it's not all right to ask for help, that asking for help would be a sign of weakness. Recovery calls for some basic changes in our thinking, and the times when we feel vulnerable are the best times to reach out and ask for help from our Higher Power, from our program, and from our friends in recovery. It's hard for us, at first. We may be afraid of rejection or of being laughed at for not knowing all the answers. But after we've taken the risk and openly asked for help, we realize our fears are a part of the past, and we can leave them behind us.

In asking for help, we acknowledge that we can't do it all by ourselves. We surrender once again to powerlessness. And we give others the joy and satisfaction of helping us.

Today if I'm feeling I'm on a "solo flight,"
help me to reach out and find support
just by asking.

Do not pray for tasks equal to your powers.
Pray for powers equal to your tasks!
— *Phillips Brooks*

What constitutes success? Is the success of a day measured in what we accomplish? In making money and advancing in our work? Or being equal to the challenge of each new day?

Recovery has made a big difference in how we think of success. To be recovering from addiction calls for a full commitment to ourselves, our relationships, our challenges, and our spiritual growth. Now, being successful means we have patience, humility, enthusiasm, and courage. The gift of recovery opens the door to these new forms of success. Our Twelve Step fellowship, our sponsor, and our new friends help us make progress. And communion with our Higher Power gives us a strength and serenity that makes us less afraid of the challenges ahead. Now, we can live a full life, "One day at a time."

Today grant me the strength to climb
each daily "mountain" and find joy
in each new vista.

*What if the choice isn't between certainties,
between this faith and that, but between faith
and* doubt? *Between renouncing the mystery
and embracing it?*

— R. Scott Bakker

Sometimes we come into a recovery program totally devoid of faith in anything or anybody. We are harboring many resentments and feel that no one was there for us in our time of greatest need. Why should we believe in a Higher Power now? Many who have come before us have had this same dilemma.

These feelings are common because we are still in our addicted frame of mind. We want an answer now; we want to be healthy now. But what takes one person only a moment to accept might take another a lifetime.

Some of us may believe our Higher Power is our Twelve Step group, while others may turn to the God we have known since childhood. When we are ready, we will believe in a Power greater than ourselves, and that Power will be the concept that feels right for us. No one person has all the answers. Having faith in a Higher Power is just one stepping-stone in our recovery. But that stepping-stone becomes the very foundation of our spiritual program.

*Today I will have faith that my life
is protected by my Higher Power.*

I am weaving the linen of night and day.
— *Kabir*

As time passes and we go through each day, we weave the tapestry of our lives. There are snags in some places and lumps in others, but the overall beauty is only enhanced by these elements. The most prized works of art are those that are truly unique.

So it is with our recovery. We create the beauty of our lives just by living. We may like some areas of the weaving more than others, but it is all beautiful in relationship to the whole. When our critical eyes are too sharp, we get into trouble. When we put on our glasses of acceptance and willingness, we can see the finery that we and our Higher Power have been weaving together.

> *Today help me see life and living as an art.*
> *Help me trust that each experience is as*
> *it should be and contributes to the*
> *beauty of the whole.*

He that has patience may compass anything.
— *François Rabelais*

When we choose to live "One day at a time," one moment at a time, we regain a more accurate, balanced perspective. This form of self-love and growth is impossible during active addiction. Now by living at a slower pace, acting thoughtfully instead of simply reacting, we get better at learning to savor the simple things.

Now we can choose to abandon the stress of commuter traffic and watch the sky long enough to spot a red-tailed hawk. We can take time to notice the fall colors throughout the woods. We can go for a walk by a lake and listen for the splash of fish feeding in the water. Or we can simply smell the rain-soaked earth while on our way to an afternoon appointment. This attention to the present is a way to combat old and familiar worries and enjoy life's small wonders. Recovery challenges us to experience a purer joy, a more honest charm and magic, and it gives us the energy and clarity to appreciate all we see.

Today let me take life in small,
manageable, delightful pieces.

If we could learn even a little to like
ourselves, maybe our cruelties and
angers might melt away.
— *John Steinbeck*

From the day we're born until the day we die, we live closely, intimately, with one person: ourselves. We are our own judge and jury, often in a harsh, self-imposed "courtroom" setting.

Now, in recovery, we can take a new, honest, and loving look at ourselves. We can recognize our assets as well as our liabilities. As we become more worthy of trust, our self-respect and self-esteem grow. As we accept our Higher Power's love for us, we learn to forgive ourselves and handle our fragile selves with new care. We become our own best friend. With kindness and caring, we break through the years and layers of pain and find the joyful child who is growing into a healthy, loving adult.

Today as I grow in recovery, I pray
that I may learn to like myself better
and treat myself and others in a
healthy, cheerful way.

JULY

When you take your inventory,
don't forget your assets.
 — *Carol K.*

Part of taking a good inventory is identifying our strengths. When we concentrate only on our defects and weaknesses, we shortchange ourselves and everyone around us. All of us have assets, and taking an inventory is a good time to get in touch with them.

We need to identify the things we do well, the things we have done for others, the care we have given. We need to give ourselves credit for our healthier bodies, our clearer minds, and our new spiritual awareness. We can let ourselves feel good about these things. They are now part of us, part of who we are. And when our inventory is really complete, we can share these positive attributes with our Higher Power, ourselves, and another human being.

There is so much we can learn and much we can give ourselves by acknowledging our strengths, our assets, and our goodness. These good things are the foundation for much growth in recovery, and we can enjoy their rewards today.

Today let me remember
the good things in me.

No man is wise enough by himself.
— *Plautus*

The people in our fellowship come together with a single purpose: the desire to remain sober. We are of various backgrounds and different races. Some of us are rich, while others have no money at all. We're all so different, yet we share a common bond: we seek sobriety. Separately, the task is insurmountable, but together we are powerful in our quest. What one of us lacks in hope and strength we find by coming together within this fellowship. Each member offers a link connecting the other. Broken, the chain is useless. Together, the strength and beauty of each link is made even more powerful. We join together in a spiritual bond that transcends our differences.

Before we joined the fellowship and chose a Higher Power, isolation made our task seem overwhelming. Now, as we look around the room at smiling and caring faces, we can be grateful that in our pain we have found such strength and the wisdom we need to stay sober "One day at a time."

Today let me be humbly grateful
for my sobriety.

Everybody should be free to go very slow.
— *Robert Frost*

We've all been in a class we hated. We probably learned very little, and we did the minimum amount of work necessary.

The same holds true for forcing our loved ones into recovery. We all learn better when we are ready to be taught and more likely to go the extra mile for sobriety. In order to help a person into recovery, we must detach with love. We can turn to our Higher Power as we mourn for our friend. Our Higher Power will bring us comfort and help us let go.

Maybe our friend has reached bottom and is ready to surrender and accept help. If so, the future can look brighter almost immediately. But maybe our friend needs more time.

Our friends are ready to accept help when they surrender the need to control life. We can only pray and wait patiently while they begin their own recovery.

Today help me to "Let go and let God."

There is no fear in love; but perfect
love casteth out fear.
　　　　　—1 John 4:18 (KJV)

Fear of people is usually a fear of rejection or disapproval, often brought about by our own sense of unworthiness. Feeling we are without value, we may settle for less than we are entitled to or less than we could have. It is difficult to strive for closeness with others or to better ourselves when we believe the answer will be "no."

But as we learn to love ourselves better, we no longer fear rejection. We know that we are valuable and unique, with or without the validation of other people. We can risk being ourselves. As our spirituality grows, we feel more confident and worthy of love. We are able to face our fears with a serenity that increases every new day.

Today let me cast out fear and know
that I am worthy of love.

i thank You God . . . for everything
which is natural which is infinite
which is yes.

— *e. e. cummings*

Within any twenty-four hours free from active addiction, our answer to small and major decisions is "yes." We are experiencing life fully and courageously, regardless of outcomes. Our feelings surface and subside like light on water. The words we share loudly or in whispers are as vivid and colorful as the world surrounding us. Our new reality is a natural gift on our spiritual journey back to friendship and health. And as our active recovery fills each day with choices, duties, events, work, and play, we are often surprised by how swiftly time passes. Each minute in recovery, as long as we work our program, we are growing. Even the hard days, when we feel the old doubts and fear and pain, are days of healing. Our Higher Power has given us a new life, a new chance to say "yes" to the best in ourselves and the world.

Today let me gratefully accept
what is offered to me.

*I do not envy people who think they have
a complete explanation of the world, for
the simple reason that they are obviously
wrong.*

— *Salman Rushdie*

How often do we hope or pray for our will to be done?
We pray for riches, prestige, a certain outcome in uncertain times. We hold the idea that if we demonstrate that
we really want a certain outcome, our wishes will be
granted.

But, buried in this attitude is an assumption that we
can control the universe. We can certainly modify our
behavior and work hard toward our goals to make it more
likely they will happen, but that's all we can do. Assuming
we can control anything except ourselves is an attempt
to grant us god-like qualities.

Instead, we can share our concerns, worries, and joys
with those close to us and with our Higher Power. As we
share these concerns, we can often hear ourselves with
new insight. We come to realize that we have already
been given all we need to be happy. As we come to accept
that we are not all-knowing, we can let go of demands
and ask instead for courage and strength.

*Today let me seek growth rather
than making demands.*

Freedom is a system based on courage.
— *Charles Péguy*

Perhaps the most difficult thing to reclaim is our freedom. During active addiction, *freedom* was often a word we used to rationalize sick behavior and avoid being responsible for ourselves. We lost all hope of happiness and growth.

Now we know that true freedom comes only from the courageous act of surrender. When we accept our Higher Power's help in defeating our addiction, we discover the supreme freedom and happiness that come to one who has overcome the impossible.

With our new courage and with the help of our Higher Power, we're learning to share our freedom and happiness with others.

Today let me be grateful for the freedom
I have found in recovery.

We can move the entire mountain
one piece at a time.
— *Chinese proverb*

Few important matters are handled well in one massive sweep. After active addiction, we believed we could somehow get several months' or years' worth of recovery in just a few days. We quickly learned that recovery is a lifelong process, not an event. Yet, what we gain in recovery is well worth the wait. Our journey restores quality at a pace that allows us to appreciate it. Our difficulties become less overwhelming, and we learn to maintain balance by taking small steps. Belonging to a fellowship that helps and celebrates these changes in us enriches each level of our growth. As we strengthen our bodies, clear our minds, and find a conscious contact with our Higher Power, we feel we can start a new life.

Our course will always be determined by the small steps we take each day. Then, one day, we will look back and marvel at all that's happened and is happening in our growth. And we'll celebrate the patience we've gained in the process.

Today let me see and enjoy
the small steps I'm taking.

We're our own worst critics. By far.
—*Julie F.*

When we make amends, we often forget the person we really harmed over and over again—ourselves. Many of us mercilessly beat ourselves up. We are relentless with self-criticism. When it comes to ourselves, we are totally unforgiving.

The Twelve Steps remind us to take inventory and make amends to those we have harmed. This includes family, friends, coworkers—and also ourselves.

Now we realize we need to be gentler on ourselves. We need to be less critical. We are working a recovery program now, and things are getting better. We can lighten up. Mentally beating ourselves up creates a spiral of self-criticism and self-blame, and we don't deserve it. We can learn to recognize self-criticism and replace it with self-love. We can replace pessimism with a new optimistic appreciation for our unique selves. We find we do deserve it.

Today let me be a best friend to myself.

This life is worth living, we can say,
since it is what we make it.
— *William James*

Active addiction fogs our thinking and progressively limits our choices in life. Finally, we are left with only two choices—recovery or death. By choosing recovery, we have again opened our lives to many new options in sobriety. Sober living requires choice. Our growth depends on our ability to identify opportunity and deal with its challenges, to face life's ups and downs rather than running from them.

We also come to understand that our reality is what we make it. Things and people, places and events, are neither good nor bad until we determine their quality. This opportunity of choice gives sober living its value. Now, we can think through and determine the value of our lives. Today, we can accept the responsibility of free choice and take steps to change ourselves. Events no longer overwhelm us. We can accept challenges, work through our problems, and enjoy the benefits of our work. What we used to think of as obstacles are now new opportunities we shape with the tools of recovery.

Today let me accept challenges as just
what I need to grow in recovery.

*Everyone in your Twelve Step program
is there to help you, even the people you
can't stand, perhaps especially the people
you can't stand.*

— Michael Graubart

We don't have to like everyone we meet in our recovery program. Odds are that we won't. And not everyone will like us.

But we do learn from everyone, and our sharing touches many others. We may hear a nugget of wisdom one night from someone we've never especially liked. When we reach out to that person in turn, we feel much better about the person and about ourselves.

You may have heard that members of the same fellowship already love each other in a very special way, and it's true. But we need to nurture that love by sharing ourselves, providing support to others when we can, and respecting everyone's right to confidentiality. As we grow spiritually, we find we have more inside—and more to give to others, too.

Our program friends are important people—we may not like all of them, but we do love them in a very special way.

*Today I am grateful for the friendships I've made
in my recovery program. Help me show each person
that I am grateful for his or her help.*

The day shall not be up so soon as I,
To try the fair adventure of tomorrow.
　　　　　　　—*William Shakespeare*

Somehow, probably because of all the grim business of addiction, we became very rigid. We learned not to trust ourselves, so we became frightened of taking risks. In recovery, we have a chance to re-establish our trust. Using the tools of recovery, we can plan an adventure with confidence. Life without adventure is like a sunset with no colors.

By nature, many of us are controllers. Adventure requires us to give up a little control, and that's scary. But we can learn to let go. When we make a routine, we can ask ourselves, "Is there another way to do this?" When the chance for adventure comes, we can ask, "Why not?"

We're healthier every new day we spend in recovery. We've replaced sickness with health, insanity with sanity, and desperation with spiritual peace. Using these tools of recovery, adventure can again bring safe fun and excitement to our lives every day.

Today help me try something new.
Help me welcome, not fear, adventure.

*The marvelous thing about a good question
is that it shapes our identity as much by the
asking as it does by the answering.*
— David Whyte

We often pass up the chance to ask a question of someone because we don't want to feel stupid. In the past, we kept very busy trying to look like we were in control, trying to seem as though we already knew what we needed to know. Now, in our new awareness that we can't live life alone, there is much we need to ask. We can learn a lot from children in this area. They are so wonderfully free of inhibitions when it comes to asking questions, and, as a result, they learn. Their world expands.

We understand ourselves and others better when we ask questions, when we seek out new knowledge. We haven't experienced, studied, read about, or heard everything there is to know, so we have many questions, especially in the area of recovery. Now we know we can go ahead and ask, that it's okay, that the answer may help improve the quality of our lives. The more we search, the more we will learn, and the more serenity we will find. Like children, our minds are hungry for knowledge.

*Today help me ask questions without worrying
about looking foolish and respond to questions
in the most helpful way I can.*

Oh, the things I learned from her
When Sorrow walked with me!
— *Robert Browning Hamilton*

We may think that forgetting the past is essential for growth and peace of mind. It's a tempting idea: we'll start over again, we think, fresh and new. But if we lose that old pain, we'll also lose all that we learned. We may repeat our mistakes or make even worse ones next time. Dwelling on the past is equally dangerous. We began recovery to build a better life.

To find and maintain our balance, each area of our lives needs attention. A healthy mind in a healthy body opens us up to a fulfilled spirit. With the help of our Higher Power, we can learn to recognize and forgive our past mistakes while we keep the remarkable lessons we learned from life.

With our remembering, with our inventory, we can truly experience the repentance that frees us from regret and remorse. When we acknowledge our mistakes, we can learn from them and come to forgive ourselves.

Today help me use my memories to learn
and change. Help me to forgive my past.

*Trouble is a part of life, and if you don't share
it, you don't give the person who loves you a
chance to love you enough.*

— *Dinah Shore*

Just as gravity keeps us grounded and connected to the
earth, our fellowship keeps us bound to sobriety. The fellowship available to us in our Twelve Step program keeps
us in reality. A problem pondered in isolation seems
immense; the same problem shared by those who truly
understand is manageable. We need other people from
the moment we are born. We need to be included, to
feel we're a part of something larger than ourselves. Our
spirits hunger for contact from others and thirst for a
relationship with our Higher Power.

Our fellowship is there, a warm, friendly, and accepting family. Our Higher Power is there. We are not alone,
no matter where we travel, no matter how large our
problems seem at the moment. Our joys are doubled
and our sadness diminished through the sharing of our
hearts.

*Today help me listen carefully and give
as well as take so I may fully experience
this gift of fellowship.*

Respect starts with yourself.
— *Anonymous*

In the midst of active addiction, the drug dictates how we relate to others: on good days, overly cautious, boastful, effusive; on bad days, nasty, negative, rude, sometimes cruel. Recovery means being aware that others are affected by our behavior and that only abstinence grants us the freedom to choose our actions.

When we first go into recovery, we are terrified by the openness we feel emotionally. We often feel wide open to others. We don't have the drugs to hide behind. We don't have a way to manipulate our moods and to make sure we are acting in the "right" manner. It is a new feeling, and often frightening, to realize that our moods have been so manipulated by our using.

But as our spiritual life grows, we find a new peace. We learn to trust ourselves and others in a new way. With the help of our Higher Power and others in recovery, we become confident that our love and good intentions are lasting. Our love, joy, and sharing are beginning to seem real and straight from the heart. Soon, we will feel proud of the way we treat others.

Today give me the courage to treat other people
the way I would like to be treated.

*You alone can get well, but you can't
get well alone.*

— *Donald A. Tubesing*

Each of us is responsible for our own well-being. We cannot blame anyone else for the progress, or lack of it, that we may experience in our efforts to change or to work a program of recovery. We alone are responsible.

But being the sole owner of responsibility for our lives does not mean we play solo! We take responsibility for our own program of recovery but link our spirits with others who also know how to recover. It's especially important in early recovery to be with those who know the ropes, who have gained the spiritual peace we hope to attain. They can guide us, support us, laugh and cry with us, and sometimes be firm with us when we seem to be heading the wrong way. All Twelve Step programs use the word "we" in each of the Steps. Recovery is not lonely. It happens in community, with others.

*Today give me the courage to join those
who are in recovery. Help me see others in
recovery as friends who know what I've
been through and want to help me.*

*Running away may relieve our anxieties
momentarily, but lasting ease requires
our turning toward what we dread most.
In dealing with fear, the way out is in.*
— *Sheldon Kopp*

Fear is a monster that is always at our backs until we turn to face it. Looking our dread in the face renders it powerless. It is not possible to be panic-stricken and honestly confront our fear at the same time.

Fear avoids sunlight and nurtures itself only in the dark corners of our lives. Taking our biggest fears out of the closet and exposing them earns us ten giant steps forward in the healing process.

We watch our fears lose their power one by one and fall away when exposed to the light of day. Sharing our secrets and fears with another human being, our sponsor, and, in some cases, our group is like walking across a dark room and turning the light on. Often we find that the shadow in the corner has disappeared.

*Today let me risk finding a safe person
to tell some of my fears and secrets to.*

This is a wonderful day. I've never
seen this one before.
— *Maya Angelou*

Although the Twelve Steps were conceived in the United States, their benefits are being felt worldwide. There are now groups all over the world—from Mexico, to India, to New Zealand, and beyond. Treatment centers, Twelve Step programs, and support for recovery are springing up everywhere. It thrills us to think of our partners in recovery in cities and countries around the world, not just around the corner.

Though we may never meet our spiritual counterparts in faraway places, we have plenty of opportunities for connection in our daily lives. In ways big and small, we can do our part to make sure the network of recovery support continues to grow every day.

Today I am grateful for the abundance
of recovery resources both close by
and far away.

We are betrayed by what is false within.
— *George Meredith*

From the beginning of our lives we were taught to control ourselves. We were taught to be strong, not to cry, and not to show others how we feel. We became false, to others and to ourselves.

But today, in recovery, we can unlearn all those teachings. Recovery demands that we let our feelings out, be honest, and share our fears. We have to let go of our old ways. Just as we learned our old lessons well, we are capable of unlearning and replacing them with our program.

We have the tools and support to learn a new, honest way of living. We can learn to recognize dishonesty. Our minds are clear again. We can finally be honest, inside and out. With nothing to hide, we can safely share our deepest secrets, our darkest fears. We can get in touch with who we really are, secure in the knowledge that our Higher Power will help us find the strength we need to change. Now, we can become real.

Today help me learn a new way
of life, "One day at a time."

Hold fast to dreams
For if dreams die
Life is a broken-winged bird
That cannot fly.
— *Langston Hughes*

The promises of Twelve Step recovery become our dreams come true. In the early stages of our sobriety, we may fear economic insecurity or have a poor self-image. It is common during the first days, months, and years of restoration to meet decision-making with self-doubt and second-guessing. By nurturing our faith in the promises of our program, we maintain the courage to continue moving forward, keeping our dreams alive and reachable. On our bad days, when our own faith may falter, we can pray for the willingness to accept the faith of others in our fellowship.

We are no longer alone in our dreams. By sharing our dreams, doubts, and pain with others, and by conscious contact with our Higher Power, we are not only growing, but we are already enjoying one of the fruits of recovery—the end of isolation. And in this environment of love and acceptance, our spirits soar and our dreams are reborn.

Today help me share my feelings
and focus on my dreams.

*"Thank you" is the best prayer that anyone could
say. I say that one a lot. "Thank you" expresses
extreme gratitude, humility, understanding.*
— Alice Walker

There are those who question whether a Higher Power
exists. But, regardless of our level of certainty or skepti-
cism, one irrefutable truth is that we are here today, no
longer in the grip of active addiction.

As hard as recovery often is, we can always be grateful
for how far we've come. We now have a program, people
who support us, a chance to build a new life. Isn't that
progress over where we were—our days of drinking,
drugging, compulsive sex, binge eating, or gambling?
In the end, we find the change in our lives was brought
about not through our own willpower but through surrender. We also find that our spirituality has nothing to
do with moralism or judgment but rather acceptance.

When we feel a need to measure how far we've come,
we need only look at where we are today—in treatment,
in a group, reading this book, thinking about recovery.
Our bodies are strong and healthy, our minds focused
and capable, and our faith has been renewed. Active
addiction is moving into our past and making way for a
joyful recovery ahead.

Today help me to recognize how far I've come.

*First keep the peace within yourself, then you
can also bring peace to others.*
— *Thomas à Kempis*

One of the things that seemed to take a good portion
of our time during active addiction was minding everybody's business but our own. We had an opinion on every
subject, knew all the details of other people's lives, and
could solve all their problems, "if only they would let
me!" Why was it, then, that we had so much trouble
in our own lives? Our Twelve Step program teaches us
we'd been trying to control everyone else's life because
we knew we couldn't control our own. Accepting this
fact and turning our thoughts inward started us thinking
about our own backyards. The more we learned about
ourselves, the less we felt a need to control others. In
short, we learned how to responsibly mind our own
business.

Now, when we find ourselves trying to solve the problems of other people, we can ask ourselves, "Am I more
interested in others because I don't want to work on my
own issues?" This gentle reminder will help us get our
thoughts back on track. And when the time comes to
offer genuine help to another, we can be sure we'll do it
humbly and out of true concern.

Today let me mind my own business first.

*We can try to avoid making choices
by doing nothing, but even that is a
decision.*

— *Gary Collins*

Now, with destructive behaviors and substances gone from our lives, we have our choices back. While we can't choose our feelings, we can choose our behavior, and isn't that a relief? If we feel irritated at a driver who's going too slow, we can think the situation through and decide how to act. We could tailgate, honk our horns and carry on, or safely switch lanes and accept what we cannot change.

In dealing with spouses, colleagues, and family, we now have the sober mind and time to stop, think, and act, rather than reacting whenever someone pushes our buttons.

Making choices again can be a little unnerving because we're rusty at it, but it also brings great freedom. No one wants to feel controlled, and that's exactly how it feels when we let others determine our behavior. We open our lives up to a full range of responses when we stop trying to control or to punish others with our anger. In making responsible choices, we find real freedom.

*Today let me accept responsibility
for how I behave.*

We don't have to know everything, and we don't have to try to manage everyone in our lives so they behave to our liking, and we don't have to stand behind the planet and push it to make sure it turns as we think it should turn.

— *Marya Hornbacher*

Our urges to get others to do what we want them to do raises a very important question about our happiness and how we achieve it. They suggest that our satisfaction in life comes from outside ourselves, from having others always react the way we would like them to react. When others don't react the way we want, we are outraged and disappointed. Life can be frustrating if our satisfaction always depends on how people react to us.

On the other hand, if we let go of the need to control others or the need to have others always react and behave as we would have them react and behave, life is a lot easier and certainly less frustrating! Then, satisfaction comes from doing the best we are able to do in life and not from how others react to us. Learning to let go takes time and faith in our Higher Power. But it is central to our recovery and peace of mind. Being responsible for our own lives now brings joy and freedom.

Today help me lead my life as best I can and let others do the same with their lives.

I have seen much to hate here—
much to forgive.
　　　　　— *Alice Duer Miller*

Some of us grew up in very sick families, and it's hard to put the past behind us. Coming to terms with who we are and learning to forgive are complicated by old pain, a childhood filled with anger and resentment and sadness. As we got older, we may have been hurt and betrayed by people we called friends. But we're not children anymore. Nor are we consumed by active addiction. We now have mature tools to use in resolving old pain. In recovery, we can learn to recognize our anger and begin to work at forgiveness.

Our past can never change, but how we view the past can. This work takes thought, tears, honesty, admitting our own mistakes, and lots of spiritual support from our group. A strong belief in a Higher Power helps reassure us that life can be good to us if we are good to ourselves. When we are finally ready to release ourselves from the past, we have truly broken free. It is a long and emotional journey but one that will release us from old pain and let us rejoice in the here and now.

Today help me learn from
the past, not live in it.

And we are put on earth a little space,
That we may learn to bear the beams of love
— *William Blake*

Since addiction robs us of the ability to love ourselves and share that love with others, it's no wonder we enter sobriety full of longing. We have come to live by unhealthy rules: "Don't talk, don't trust, don't feel." These survival skills helped us withstand active addiction, but now they are obstacles keeping us from full recovery, and we must change them. This isn't easy. No matter how much pain and isolation our old ways have brought to our lives, they are familiar ways, and attraction to the familiar is hard to resist. As unhealthy as we were in every way, we may sometimes long for comfort and predictability in our lives.

Healthy love seems risky. It can be a fearsome task to open ourselves to another, to risk shame and rejection. Healthy love requires honesty and faith, careful attention to our feelings, and sharing.

But now we are physically, mentally, and spiritually ready for love. The payoff is life itself, lived and shared in the moment, and the glow of self-esteem we feel when we are accepted as we are by another.

Today grant me the willingness
to talk, trust, and feel.

Play fuels your creativity, tickles your inner
child, and nurtures your soul.
— *Claudia Black*

When we think about play, we usually think of children. They are the ones who play all day, often in carefree abandon.

But in recovery, we're realizing we need to play, too. As adults, we often find we've lost track of the ability or desire to play. We often don't know how to do it anymore. We feel stiff, self-conscious, out of place. Years of destructive cycles have buried our sense of real fun.

Sometimes we need to learn again from our own children or, if we don't have any, from a friend's children. Or, we can think back on the happy moments of our own childhood. What activities or hobbies brought us great joy? Spending an hour or a day or a weekend having sober fun is a wonderful way to get back in touch with our own inner child and our own ability to play. Play sharpens our minds, relaxes our bodies, and lets our spirits soar. When we remember how to play, we can be grateful that having fun is one of the first things we humans learn to do.

Today help me take some time to play.

We crucify ourselves between two thieves:
regret for yesterday and fear of tomorrow.
— *Fulton Oursler*

We've all said or done things we regretted. If only we could turn back the clock and have a second chance. Sadly, we don't have that power. We have to live with our words and deeds, even when we spoke or acted out of haste or in a drug-induced fog.

We can't do anything about tomorrow, either, and worrying about tomorrow robs us of today. Certainly we can prepare by doing homework, packing for a trip, or writing the speech we are to give. But once we've done the preparation, it's time to let go.

But today is ours. We can make amends, see someone in person and say, "I'm sorry," or send a card with a note of apology. We can think about what we could do differently in the future. And we can ask for guidance from our Higher Power. We can't erase what we said or did, but we can speak or act differently today.

Taking life "One day at a time" means living in today, in the here and now. Living in the past or future is futile. Instead, we can cherish this moment, relax, and enjoy it.

Today help me to let go of the troubles
of the past and the fears of tomorrow.
Help me make the most of today.

My heart is a lonely hunter
that hunts on a lonely hill.
— Fiona MacLeod

Recovery asks us to live each day responsibly, but defining responsibility can be difficult. Many of us knew little about mature, disciplined, fulfilling lifestyles. Our original families may have been damaged, our parents unavailable as sources of nurturing. How, then, do we choose a new path? We begin by asking for help from our Higher Power when we are unsure or in pain. Next, we think through our choices, guided by the knowledge we've gained. And finally, we act.

We know, for instance, that we've returned to an active level of our illness when we recognize the ache of isolation. At that point, it is our responsibility to call someone, share our feelings, and ask advice. Next, we call on our spiritual growth to help us be honest and act on the advice we get. When we do this, we are practicing self-love, we are growing, and we are taking control of what we can do to change our lives.

In doing these things, day by day our Higher Power will help us remove sadness and replace it with fellowship. We are giving up our isolation and becoming part of our world again.

Today let me take healthy action to eliminate
one source of pain or sadness in my life.

It's great to be great, but it's
greater to be human.
— *Will Rogers*

All of us dream and daydream about greatness. But in the end, it's greater to be human. Rich or famous people live in a different world from most people. Many wish they could just blend in with the crowd once in a while. They can't walk into a store or go to a restaurant without being bombarded by people who want their autograph or want to touch them.

The rest of us don't have to maintain a certain image. We can cry or get angry. We can be silly and say what we really mean. Being ordinary, with all its frailties and foibles, is great compared with having to live up to a certain image all the time. As average and very human beings, we can accept our bodies with all their imperfections, enjoy our flawed and quirky minds, and be grateful to our Higher Power for our blessings. And, when we humbly accept our humanity, we are all great.

Today help me accept my humanity
and remember to love myself with
all my imperfections.

AUGUST

I to myself am dearer than a friend.
— *William Shakespeare*

We can't put off telling ourselves about our goodness. It's tempting to believe we can reward ourselves only when we accomplish something remarkable. But it is remarkable to be recovering. It takes honesty and courage to work these Twelve Steps. We've been in battle; we've suffered. Now, having been there, we've learned about tolerance, forgiveness, serenity, faith, and gratitude.

We are scarred, yes, but they are scars of triumph, scars of survival. There's a level of humanity and wisdom that suffering has revealed to us. It has made us deeper, more well-rounded individuals. Having nearly lost our lives, we are more careful to increase our blessings. We don't take our physical, mental, or spiritual health for granted anymore. We actively work toward harmony and balance.

We've been given a rare gift—the chance to witness and partake in the change from sickness to health, from pain to healing, from sadness to joy, from emptiness to serenity.

Today let me compliment myself
on the fine person I'm becoming
and always was.

*I don't blame my parents. This stuff has
been handed down for generations.*
— Seth P.

Sometimes, when we begin to get better, we feel anger
and frustration with other family members who are not
in recovery. We're often quick to tell them they'd better
"get with the program" and start recovering soon.

More often than not, our words fall on deaf ears. It's
one thing to tell someone about the help and resources
that are available. It's another to expect them to instantly
understand and seek help for themselves.

Most of us come from families that have struggled
with alcoholism or other addictions for generations.
It's no one's fault. It's a source of pride, though, that we
can be part of the solution and help break the cycle of
intergenerational pain.

With help from our Higher Power, we can let go of
unrealistic expectations. We can let our loved ones find
recovery at their own pace, in their own time.

We like to carry the message of recovery to others. But
it is a message of hope, not a message of blame.

*Today I'm grateful to be in recovery
and not trapped in the pattern of
addiction or other sickness or pain.
I feel a new freedom today.*

Let me be a little kinder,
Let me be a little blinder
To the faults of those around me,
Let me praise a little more.
— *Edgar Guest*

Sometimes we find it easy to be critical of others; we find it easier to inventory another person's bad habits instead of our own. It is often a defensive posture born of low self-esteem. Not only does it waste sober time and energy, it also creates resentment and grandiosity in us, and that hurts our recovery. When we are foolish enough to criticize another's choice, we are setting ourselves up for trouble.

When we pray for the strength to praise rather than criticize, we find that praise is its own reward. We feel better, more optimistic about ourselves and our world. When we pay attention to ourselves and let others do the same, life's burden lifts, and our spirit flowers and opens so our Higher Power can work with us. We are lucky that our only life is our own. We had so much trouble handling life before recovery; one is enough for us now. And now we can make that life a rich one.

Today let me live my own life and allow
others their rightful space to live theirs.

Don't compromise yourself;
you are all you've got.
— *Janis Joplin*

We continue to learn through our recovery program that we feel better when we listen to our feelings. Even though we may be uncomfortable when we disagree with others or refuse to go along with the crowd, we are much more peaceful when we don't do something just because everybody else is doing it. We like the part of recovery that is teaching us to be honest with ourselves and others.

Feelings are like a road map to us. Author David Viscott said they "indicate how you are reacting to the world around you." When we begin to understand our anger, guilt, anxiety, joy, hurt, and loss, we realize feelings are road markers we can use to grow in recovery. Although our feelings were dulled for years by substances and destructive patterns, we have found it is never too late to listen to our feelings and learn from what they are teaching us. It is a new language for us; it is painful sometimes but always true.

Today I pray to let others experience
the real me, including my feelings.

Laugh at yourself first, before anyone else can.
— *Elsa Maxwell*

When was the last time we had a good laugh, really laughed, until tears rolled down our cheeks and we had to catch our breath? Remember how good we felt afterward?

There is more and more evidence that laughter actually makes us feel good physically as well as emotionally. Laughter reduces muscle tension, exercises the lungs, and stimulates the circulatory system. It rejuvenates our minds and uplifts our spirits. After a good laugh we can feel calmer, rejuvenated, even younger.

A burst of clean, refreshing humor helps us to stop taking ourselves so seriously. Someone once said the next best thing to solving a problem is finding some humor in it!

People who laugh on a regular basis usually have fewer physical and emotional problems than those who find it difficult to see humor in anything. Luckily, humor is all around us if we just look for it. We can watch funny movies, read the comics in the paper, join in the giggling of our children, and choose to be with people who have a healthy sense of humor.

Humor is spiritual, and it heals.

*Today help me laugh and to nurture
my sense of humor.*

In order to live free and happily,
you must sacrifice boredom. It is
not always an easy sacrifice.
— *Richard Bach*

One luxury we simply cannot afford today is boredom. It is a condition that occurs when we lose sight of what's happening around us. When bored, we may invest in self-pity and dig ourselves into an emotional trench, unlit, lined in loneliness. Boredom can be toxic, and sometimes we can't think ourselves into doing anything. But we can get busy and "do" ourselves into thinking. While this isn't always easy at first, it gets us moving again.

And, as they say, when we "bring the body, the mind will follow." The spirit follows, too.

Soon, we are actively engaged in life again, and our attention is once more in the present. Often, simply going for a walk or washing the dishes is all we need. Our bodies are designed for movement, our senses to be stimulated, our minds to seek knowledge, and our spirits to bring us peace. When we get them started, they can carry us a long way—after all, they've carried us into a joyful new life, haven't they?

Today help me grow thankful for the
meaning that sober activity
has given my life.

That is the happiest conversation where there is no competition, no vanity, but a calm, quiet interchange of sentiments.
— *Samuel Johnson*

When we say, "We're not communicating well," often what we're really saying is, "I'm communicating just fine; it's the other person who isn't communicating well!" We tend to expect other people, especially those closest to us, to know instinctively what we want to hear.

When we talk to a loved one about our recovery, our new sober friends, and our new experiences, we may be disappointed if they don't react the way we expected. We're hurt and believe since we initiated the discussion, the other person has the communication problem.

But, we all have different styles of communication. We can't change another; we can't force someone to say the words we long to hear. We can only change ourselves. We can start by letting go of expectations. We can forgive others for not being as we'd hoped. And we can choose to share our joy in recovery with those who understand us. Sharing our feelings for the simple pleasure of self-expression can bring us great joy. In doing this, we communicate our true selves.

Today let me share honestly and without expectations.

let all go
dear
so comes love
— *e. e. cummings*

The concept of "letting go," surrendering so change will occur in our lives, is not new to us. Our addicted life required complete surrender to our drug of choice. Physical, emotional, and spiritual sacrifices were demanded of us on a daily basis. These sacrifices gained us nothing but pain and isolation and self-hate. Yet we clung to them, afraid to let go.

We still have a daily duty now, a duty to our recovery. Our most important task is to understand and accept what we cannot control—our addiction, other people, the past, the weather—and turn them over to our Higher Power.

How satisfying surrender in sobriety is today! What relief we feel when we surrender our cares, knowing that our Higher Power will help us find a new way to live. In surrender, we discover and claim serenity, fellowship, integrity, accountability, peace, focus, and love.

> *Today help me let go of at least*
> *one thing I cannot change.*

*This is the reality of being a survivor
and a person in recovery. We all have
darkness inside us that will always be
there to some degree.*

— Jennifer Storm

There are so many sides to all of us. It's not just a matter of "good" or "bad."

Perhaps this is most true within our own families. Whoever makes up our family—whether it's our children, parents, spouse, or friends—the feelings we have are often intense and contradictory.

Some of our relationships are strained. Some are improving. Where there is active addiction, everything often seems hopeless. Feelings change from day to day.

Our families can be the source of our greatest joys and our greatest pain. But in recovery, we are ready—body, mind, and spirit—to find balance in our lives. We are healthy again, able to see more clearly the shades of gray—the many sides that most people have. Now, we are learning not to think of people as "good" or "bad" but to understand, love, and accept them, and ourselves, as we are.

*Today let me focus on how much
I care about my family and how
I can tell them I care.*

Forgiveness is better than revenge; for forgiveness is the sign of a gentle nature, but revenge the sign of a savage nature.

— *Epictetus*

We remember how it felt when we plotted revenge against past enemies. If we are honest with ourselves, we probably will remember feelings of anger, power, control, and frustration. If the actual vengeful act was carried out, we probably then experienced more anger, more frustration, and more pain.

These feelings have no place in a successful recovery. They inhibit our growth by keeping alive our past guilt, envy, and anger. Now that we have come to learn the wisdom of a Twelve Step approach to life, we can see the folly of revenge. This cannot be positive when our feelings are so destructive.

Forgiveness grants us a different kind of power. It gives us a chance to experience kindness, understanding, and humility. We become gentle in nature and more able to use our minds for positive change. We can recognize the destructive powers of vengeful thoughts and work to change. We can understand why people have hurt us and learn to forgive. In forgiveness, we heal and we are healed.

Today let me build a friendship
with forgiveness.

A child is fed with milk and praise.
— *Mary Lamb*

When we were children, we probably had needs that were not met. Maybe we needed more attention—maybe we got too much of the wrong kind. Maybe no one encouraged us the way we think they should have. That little boy or girl who needed something is still in us. Even though we're grown, that history, that past, is still part of us, and we need to nurture our child within.

We can do this by remembering we're no longer helpless and by taking action to make life good for ourselves. We're at a perfect place to change our lives—our spirits, our minds, and our bodies are healthy, safe, and sound. We can rekindle the joys of childhood. Perhaps some childlike play, a hobby, or music will do it. Even if we think we're no good at singing or drawing, the more we do it, the more we let ourselves enjoy it, and the closer we grow to that inner child. We can't do anything about our childhood, but we can, at last, get the love we need—from ourselves and others.

Today let me take time to enjoy some play.

*We can complain because rose bushes
have thorns or rejoice because thorn
bushes have roses.*

— *Anonymous*

Reasons for gratitude are easy to find. If we're breathing, we can think of people hooked up to oxygen tanks. If our skin is smooth, we can remember people suffering in burn units. If we ran into a store for a minute to buy a gallon of milk today, we can remember the long lines people in other countries endure for the same errand.

And we exist! That alone is miraculous! We have survived a chronic, often fatal disease. For many of us, life is better than before addiction, because we've found a new appreciation for life, a new depth and peace, a new calmness. And we can continue to grow in recovery each beautiful day that is given to us. Around the world today, thousands of babies are being born, and many people like us are finding renewed recovery. Millions of new, hopeful, and exciting possibilities are arriving every day.

Now, we're ready to take our place in the sun as one of the world's new and hopeful possibilities.

*Today let me look for the good
in my world and be thankful.*

You are never given a wish without also being given the power to make it come true. You may have to work for it, however.

— *Richard Bach*

Staying free of harmful substances and behaviors is sometimes more difficult than simply stopping. Our sobriety is a gift, but it isn't free. To recover, we need a plan of action and a willingness to work. If we take the Twelve Steps and group them by threes, we can see that we will "give up," "clean up," "make up," and "grow up." If we suffer a setback in one area, we can work on those Steps with our sponsor. Sometimes we reach another level of growth in our recovery; then we can go back and work the Steps in a new way. So we start again, as beginners, but with all the mental skills and clarity we've developed in sobriety. Safe in the care of our Higher Power, we've begun to dream again. And our physical selves have begun to recover, too; they will take us where we want to go.

Success comes in doing, moving forward, one step at a time. When we wish for and work at sobriety, we find our possibilities are endless.

Today grant me the willingness to dedicate effort toward the gift of sobriety.

> *To love one's self is the beginning*
> *of a lifelong romance.*
> — *Oscar Wilde*

People who value themselves take good care of themselves. The better care we give ourselves, the healthier we become and, in turn, the more we value ourselves. Since most of us have difficulty feeling valuable, we can start to improve our self-esteem by taking good care of ourselves. It's the little things, like putting some pretty color on our nails or enjoying a soothing bath instead of a shower. Making a complete, healthy meal for ourselves to nourish our bodies will help our self-esteem. Spending time with friends or a quiet time with our Higher Power can also help.

Sometimes we may want to feel low. We may actually want to believe we are not worth great care. This is sad, and it's not sobriety. Sobriety is doing the things that are healthy, even if we'd rather not. It means eating a balanced diet and getting enough rest, exercising our minds, and embracing a spiritual way of life. It's a lot of work, but soon the payoff begins: we feel lovable, worthwhile, happy, and hopeful again.

> *Today let me do one small,*
> *nice thing for myself.*

Awake, my soul! Stretch every nerve,
And press with vigor on;
A heavenly race demands thy zeal,
And an immortal crown.
— *Philip Doddridge*

By making the choice to get sober, we also accept the fact that we won't be an instant success. Accepting our illness doesn't end our addiction but gives us the chance to deal with it. Relief from the burden of compulsions frees our potential and grants us distance from the pain of our old lifestyle.

Now, while we expect no medal for winning the race, we are offered the chance to run. Addiction created a life lived in hell, filled with anger, hatred, resentment, and mistrust. But now another way of living is slowly unfolding. We can set to work creating a spiritual life, one in which we honor our bodies, our minds, and our spirits. The race is never finished, but now we are in it. With the help of our Twelve Step program and our Higher Power, we are confident of our future.

Today let me remember that I can do
whatever I need to do.

*When we get sober, we may have
a lot to learn about what kinds of
pleasure we like.*

— *Jennifer Matesa*

Our sexuality is colored by our past experiences and our expectations for the future. Our sexuality is also influenced by social factors: advertisements, talk shows, movies, songs, and more. With all these influences, it's not surprising that most of us are somewhat confused and often disappointed in our own sexuality.

If we're newly recovering, "Easy does it" is the best thing to remember. When we were tied to our compulsive behaviors, we may have abused our sexuality. We may have used it as a weapon or threat. We may have allowed others to abuse it. We may have acted in ways we never would have sober. Recognizing this, we must now forgive ourselves and make a serious commitment to respect our bodies. Our Higher Power can help us let go of our past mistakes.

Making peace with our sexuality can help us value and enjoy ourselves again. Slowly, in time, positive feelings about our bodies and ourselves as sexual beings will develop.

*Today I pray that my sexual self
will emerge healthy and proud.*

*The longer you're in recovery, the more
you appreciate humor.*

—*Julie K.*

Humor has long been recognized as an aid to recovery.
Humor is part of most Twelve Step meetings in one form
or another. With practice, we can often find humor in
our past mistakes, our current situation, and our hopes
and fears for the future. We appreciate humor because
it shows our common bond. It brings our spirits closer
together. It relieves tension and helps us banish worry. We
laugh as a group—never *at* someone but *with* someone.

Humor also gives us a way to share an experience we
all know only too well. When we smile or laugh, we own
our pain, forgive ourselves, and share understanding.

We may have lost our sense of humor from years of
seriousness, neglect, inner pain, and rigidity. Regaining
it can be a sign that we are making real progress in our
recovery after years of pain, hurt, and isolation. The
smiles humor generates remind us that we are getting
better every day.

*Today let me share laughter
with another person.*

We must be willing to begin
to learn to love ourselves.
— *Louise Hay*

What a joy, what a relief to find a new friend in recovery—ourselves. Long hidden, perhaps to the point of nonexistence, we buried ourselves in years of drugs and addictive behaviors and denied our own presence as a participant in life. Rediscovering ourselves doesn't happen overnight, however, just because we halt our destructive cycles. It's a gradual getting-to-know-you process.

It takes time, patience, and tender loving care to establish a relationship with ourselves and to come to believe in ourselves again. It also takes discipline. Our bodies need nourishment, sleep, and exercise. Our minds crave nourishment, too. And our spirit requires daily prayer, meditation, or connection with our Higher Power to flourish.

But, the rewards are great. Now we can look forward to spending a lifetime with someone we love: ourselves.

Today help me see myself as a whole person,
worthy of love, care, and respect as I grow
in sobriety. Help me accept who I am
and become the best I can be.

Peace and joy.
— *Bill M.*

One Twelve Step friend closes a visit or conversation by wishing us "peace and joy." It's a simple blessing, but what more could anyone want than peace and joy?

Peace comes from knowing we've tried our best to love and care about ourselves and others, that we've tried our best to make the world a better place, and that we have supportive relationships, including one with our Higher Power. Being perfect is not a prerequisite to finding peace. In fact, perfectionism usually destroys any chance of peace.

When we are at peace with ourselves, our Higher Power, and the world, joy follows. There is joy in welcoming another sunrise or sunset. There is joy in a phone call from a friend, in going to a meeting, in telling someone "I love you." Nothing fancy, elaborate, or grand—just simple peace and joy. How wonderful to have them, even if only for a few minutes, hours, or days. Sobriety has a wonderful way of helping these things happen.

> *Today may I find peace and joy*
> *in my recovery, and may I share*
> *them and wish them for others.*

When I lose my Higher Power, I always
find Him in the garden.

— Jill H.

During active addiction, our spiritual lives were bankrupt. We knew only our own tiny corner of the universe,
and it was usually a grim one. We were alone and lost.
Now, in recovery, we find a great gift: a chance to develop
a whole new relationship with a Higher Power. This can
strengthen and sustain us during the worst of times and
fill our lives with love every day.

Once, we doubted the existence of anything positive
and loving. We felt if there were a Higher Power, it must
be a cruel and vindictive force. Now, everywhere we
look, we see positive forces at work.

For many of us, prayer and meditation have become
the most important and satisfying parts of our recovery
program. As we discover the rituals that help us feel
connected to our spiritual selves, we can work to inte-
grate them into our daily routines. Time with our Higher
Power in the morning helps us start the day with calm
confidence, instead of confusion and anxiety. Meditation
during the day helps us recontact our spiritual selves and
leave petty concerns behind us. And prayer before sleep
brings us peace to end our day. These are all parts of our
newfound spirituality.

Today I will be grateful to my Higher Power
for bringing light and joy to my life.

Give us the tools and we will finish the job.
— *Winston Churchill*

Addiction is a disease without prejudice; no one is immune. But the tools of recovery are available for anyone, too. Anyone with a desire to remain sober and live a healthy life can experience the joys of recovery.

Identifying our dreams for the future and asking for our Higher Power's help to achieve them is an important part of recovery. This conscious contact with a Power greater than ourselves brings peace to our spirit and helps us overcome the struggles ahead. Accepting that we will be shown the way, even when we are tempted to stray, brings us serenity as we face the hard work of recovery.

The common bond we share with our sponsor and Twelve Step fellowship—a bond of friendship, faith, and experience—can support us and provide the help we need to face each new day.

All of us have the tools we need to find serenity: honesty to help defeat denial, faith to conquer fear and uncertainty, sponsorship and fellowship to end our isolation, and communion with our Higher Power to grant us peace.

Today help me use all the tools available to me
to make real progress in my recovery.

My relationships depend on being honest with other people. My life depends on being honest with myself.

—Angela L.

Before our recovery from addiction, we didn't know what honesty was. We thought honesty meant not getting caught. We used honesty like money, spending just enough to get through the day.

But in recovery, we can regain our integrity. Now we can think clearly and know it's important to be honest with other people and even more important to be honest with ourselves. Once, we could convince ourselves that our lives were in great shape, or that our problems were someone else's, and keep using.

But we don't deny our problems anymore. And we know that when we lie to ourselves, we are hurting our recovery. We don't like ourselves very much, then, and need to escape—back to our drug of choice.

Before, being dishonest didn't matter; we had nothing to lose. Now we've regained our health—physically, mentally, and spiritually. Dishonesty could cost us everything, even our lives. But now we also have our program, we have each other, and we have our Higher Power to remind us every day of the freedom honesty can bring.

Today let me look in a mirror and see an honest person looking back.

Every day is a holiday.
— *Anonymous*

The janitor in a school was an extremely positive, spiritual person. When asked how his day was going, he said in a loud, cheerful voice, "Every day is a holiday." When overloaded by work or family schedules, what a great thought to remember. Every day is a holiday!

The original meaning of "holiday" was simply a happy or festive day, a day to celebrate, to rejoice, to give thanks. In recovery, every day is a holiday—something special. Each day is a gift, given by a Power greater than ourselves, to use as we choose. What a change from active addiction, when every day was misery.

Thinking of each day as special helps us to be grateful and to give thanks for every day in our new lives. As we grow in recovery, we look forward to every day with joy and excitement.

Thanks for today. Let me live it as a holiday,
a day to celebrate recovery and sobriety.

*It's only those who do nothing
that make no mistakes.*
— *Joseph Conrad*

A sense of humor is one part of us that is rescued by recovery from the dulled life of addiction. Laughter heals us and separates us from suffocating false pride. As we mend emotions, we gladly let go of our need to be right all the time. We move away from that old, fearful defensiveness, and we come to accept our mistakes. It is endearing when we relate to one another as a result of our human imperfections. This is the spiritual path we have chosen over self-centered preoccupation.

When we laugh we are truly living in the moment. We are freeing ourselves from our worries, if only for a moment. As humans, we are lucky to be one of only a few species on Earth that have the ability to recognize and appreciate humor. Laughter relieves the pressure of a closed mind. Laughter reminds us that our mistakes are not disasters but simply by-products of our growth.

*Today let me share laughter over
my mistakes with another person.*

You've got to make a conscious choice
every day to shed the old—whatever
"the old" means for you.
— *Sarah Ban Breathnach*

To surrender our own will may at first seem like giving up life itself. It seems so risky to relinquish control! We may resist at first and desperately look for an easier, softer way, before we realize we must simply surrender. In time, we come to believe our Higher Power can be trusted to comfort and support us, to bring order into our lives on a day-by-day, minute-by-minute basis. Before, we lived in chaos and felt terribly alone. In recovery, we can find calm and safety when we surrender our will and our lives to our Higher Power. We can witness the powerfully positive results every day. Now the real healing begins.

Today I will be aware of the influence
of my Higher Power in my life. I will
risk letting go of control and trusting
in a Power greater than myself.

Trust is the answer to doubt. We have a habit of thinking one must trust in something, as if trust were not a perfectly solid thing, a perfectly good noun, unto itself.

— *Marya Hornbacher*

After everything we experienced in active addition, it may be difficult for us to believe in anything. Maybe we grew up learning about a concept of God or religion but that concept no longer speaks to us. Maybe we have never felt in touch with ourselves as spiritual beings.

We now see that our efforts to control our own lives have not been successful. We also see that many aspects of our lives have improved greatly in recovery. In moments when we have trouble believing that anyone or anything is watching over us, it can be helpful to just remember those simple truths.

How would we act today if we weren't controlled by doubt? What difference would it make to simply accept that our life has improved, even though it may never be perfect? Can we let go of needing explanations and simply trust?

Today let me accept the imperfections in my life and trust that recovery is the right path.

Humility, that low, sweet root,
From which all heavenly virtues shoot
— *Thomas Moore*

When we try to build our self-confidence by believing we are better than others, we usually fall flat on our faces. Making ourselves feel bigger at the expense of another human being can only end in disaster and loneliness. Grandiosity creates distance from our fellows. It takes a lot of energy to keep proving that we are better than others. Somehow our victories in self-righteousness feel hollow because, deep down inside, we really feel like we are faulty.

As we regain our health, we find we don't need to judge others in order to feel good about ourselves.

When we feel separate and want to reconnect with others, our program of recovery helps us learn the words that bring us back. "I need help," "I'm sorry," and "I understand" are powerful ways to share humanity and be a part of the real world again.

Today let me abandon my pride and
refrain from judging others. Help me
find my own good feelings.

Today is ours, to do with as we will.
— *Richmond Walker*

Recovery means we can make choices on a daily basis, choices that will be in our best interests. Now, we can choose to be loving, forgiving, and positive. We can choose the people, places, and things that bring comfort and joy to our lives. Now, we can choose life.

In recovery, we have tools to help us make these choices: our Twelve Step program, sober friends, slogans, and literature. We have a new physical and mental stamina to help us make and fulfill healthy decisions. And our spiritual rebirth gives us serenity and peace no matter what problems we may face.

We are saying goodbye to our past, and we can't look into the future. We can only work on ourselves today.

*Today guide my choices as I lead a
sober life, "One day at a time."*

Adopt the pace of Nature:
her secret is patience.
— *Ralph Waldo Emerson*

One of the mixed blessings of early recovery from addiction is the remarkable healing power of the human body. Except for those in the late stages of addiction, most of us begin to feel better fairly quickly, often within a few days. But complete physical recovery from an addiction to a substance takes a long time. Emotional and spiritual recovery usually takes longer.

We can easily get discouraged when our emotional and spiritual recovery lags so far behind the physical.

Most crucial to our recovery, especially early recovery, is patience. We need to have patience with family and friends who may not understand that we have an illness called addiction. We need patience with Twelve Step group members who may sometimes move too fast or seem not to understand us. Above all, we need patience with ourselves. Our Higher Power can help us learn to love ourselves, even when we seem to be moving slowly.

Recovery takes time. We do what we can and let time and our Higher Power do their share of the healing.

Today let me be patient. Help me know
that, like a plant, recovery will grow
within me if I nurture it.

I can hear music . . . sweet, sweet music.
— *Brian Wilson*

We often find it helpful to think about the role music has played in our lives. Sometimes, it has been a problem for us: time spent listening to loud, blaring music was a time of physical and emotional isolation, usually under the influence of drugs.

In recovery, we may find ourselves drawn to a different kind of music, something that speaks to our changing way of life. Perhaps it is more soothing or relaxing. Perhaps it has lyrics that give us a new perspective. Perhaps it is a new artist.

Whatever type of music we choose, we find it is much more than a pastime for us. It is an appreciation. Our favorite artists, our favorite songs: some never change, some do.

Our relationship with music is growing and changing. In recovery, we find music engages our minds and relaxes our bodies in a new way. Music lifts our spirits, too. We are grateful that music is part of our lives and that we now have a chance to think about it and perhaps even develop some new interests. Music is an excellent way to get to know other people, helps us unwind after a hard day, and adds a new dimension to our enjoyment of life.

*Today I give thanks for music. Help me
to love and appreciate it even more
now that I am sober.*

To come to possess all,
desire the possession of nothing.
— *St. John of the Cross*

Expectations can cause havoc in our daily living. We all have a basic right to be treated with dignity and respect, but that doesn't mean life will always go our way. The twists and turns of life often carry us up rivers of disappointment to shores we never chose to visit.

Facing life as fully involved travelers, without expectations about outcomes, is perhaps the brightest way to travel. Making plans without setting up for certain outcomes makes us flexible people who learn to go with the flow. It has been said that there is a direct proportion between our level of expectation and the amount of stress we have in our lives. Trusting the results to a larger plan allows us to relax and enjoy the adventure of the journey.

As we grow closer to our Higher Power, we find we can let go. We are more peaceful and confident, less frantic and controlling. Trusting that our Higher Power will protect us, no matter what we encounter on our journey, helps us face the future with a calm and loving heart.

Today let me relax into life and
let go of my expectations.

SEPTEMBER

Spirituality is an individual matter.
I can tell you what it means to me,
but it might be different for you.
— *Jake T.*

Many of us get confused when we begin to talk about religion and spirituality. We hear newcomers ask if the two are the same. If they aren't, how are they different?

Perhaps the simplest explanation is this one: you can be spiritual but not necessarily religious. Or you can be religious and spiritual. But being religious doesn't necessarily mean you are also a spiritual person.

Our spirituality is clearly reflected in our daily lives: how we treat others, how we treat ourselves. Are we honest? Caring? Sharing? Do we listen? Do we have time for other people?

For many of us, spirituality does not come easy. Our feelings have been numbed by alcohol, food, and other substances. We lost touch with our faith and became isolated from the world. We were left with a tremendous inner void. Now, we're learning that spirituality can help us fill it. Our spiritual growth is one sure signpost on the road to recovery.

Today guide me to find what spirituality
means to me. Help me become
a spiritual person.

*Today I will focus on what's right about
me. I will give myself some of the caring
I've extended to the world.*

— *Melody Beattie*

Overcommitment is a juggling act in which we try to
keep several balls in the air at once. We juggle our job,
family, and self-care responsibilities at a furious speed
until we tire or feel overwhelmed. When we feel overwhelmed, the first ball we usually drop is self-care, prom-
ising ourselves we will pick it up again "when we have
time."

But we can easily change the pace and speed of our
act instead of neglecting our personal needs. Nothing
feels better than being well-rested and physically and
emotionally fit. When we remember how it feels to be in
great condition, we wonder why we ever stopped taking
good care of ourselves.

Today, we can begin to get our priorities straight again
and put our own needs at the top of our daily list. If we
love ourselves enough to make self-care a top priority,
everything else will fall into place.

*Today let me remember that I can give to others
only if I also nurture my own needs.*

Let the events about to come, come!
— *Kabir*

If we stay open to the will of our Higher Power, everything happens as it should. Sometimes we don't understand or can't get the "big picture." Since we can't see into the future, we can become angry and resentful with the way events are unfolding. We're sure we know a better way. This grandiosity can lead to the loss of both our serenity and our acceptance of our powerlessness. We want to change the things we can't, which leads to frustration and general ill will.

Do we really trust our Higher Power? Can we be patient and accept that we will learn the meaning of events as we need to, not as we want to? If so, we can live for today. We will be given only what we can handle in each day. We needn't project and worry about tomorrow or yesterday. We are beginning to trust our Higher Power in a new way by letting go of the need to have everything explained to us before it is permitted to happen. We know our Higher Power will guide us through the events that are to come.

> *Today I will welcome the day and the*
> *opportunities to grow and learn what*
> *my Higher Power has in store for me.*

The two most powerful warriors are patience
and time: *they will do everything.*
— *Leo Tolstoy*

When we look at the patterns in our lives, it seems that
doors open and events happen at exactly the right time.
Even when we don't think so, even when it seems that
the worst thing happens at the worst possible moment,
the universe is operating perfectly. Letting the current
of life carry us along works better than swimming
upstream. When the time for change is near, the forces
of nature seem to be cooperative and we find ourselves
at the right place.

It is frustrating to feel ready for change but stuck in a
seemingly unchanging situation. Sometimes we feel that
we have been forgotten when our Higher Power doesn't
bring us what we think we want, when we want it. Trust,
patience, and a wider vision can be our best friends as
we wait for the right door to open.

*Today let me realize that I am exactly where
I'm supposed to be at this moment.*

Come forth into the light of things,
Let Nature be your teacher.
— *William Wordsworth*

When life seems filled with stress, nature can help us find harmony among body, mind, and spirit. Walking on the beach on a Sunday morning, listening to the sound of the waves crashing against the breakwater, we can hear our own thoughts, and all of life, more clearly.

When we jog, the rhythm of our steps and the fresh air draw us inward. We form a closer relationship with our inner self. Complex problems take on simpler dimensions and our confidence grows.

At times like these, we feel a profound intimacy with our Higher Power and the best that is in us. Our new awareness of nature's simplicity and harmony brings us a great sense of peace and well-being. Confident in our Higher Power's presence, we can face the future with serenity.

Today help me feel close to nature. Help me
find harmony in all areas of my life.

We can create our own path and our own sacred place where we can be silent and just observe, letting our senses bathe in how good it is to be alive, free of our addiction.

— *Victor La Cerva*

Often it feels impossible to get away from the hectic nature of human life. As soon as one task is over, we are compelled to begin on the next. It's no wonder that we can feel overwhelmed. Fortunately, we can always create a mental break for ourselves when we need it. Sometimes just sitting still and saying "please help me" will bring us a blessed feeling of peace and relief.

When we take a moment to collect our thoughts and remember the goodness that recovery has brought us, our whole outlook improves. But then we seem to forget again and rush about.

Maybe we can find a way to tie a mental string around our finger to remind us that every problem we have has a spiritual solution. When we become overwhelmed again, we could try turning to a favorite slogan or mantra, taking a walk in our favorite park, or just closing our eyes and enjoying a minute of mental quiet right where we are. The more we practice pausing and letting go, the safer life becomes.

Today help me remember that a moment of peace is always there when I need it.

Be not afraid of life. Believe that life
is worth living, and your belief will
help create the fact.

— William James

Once in a while, when everything seems to be going wrong in life, it is normal to feel like we should just give up. But it is dangerous to nurture that feeling. Many things can and do go wrong, even in recovery. Someone else gets the job or promotion we were expecting. We break up with our partner. A loved one falls ill.

When things go wrong, the question often raised is, "What's the use? We do our best, work hard, go to meetings, but things still go wrong, so what's the use?"

The answer is in our attitude. If we believe everything should always go our way, we will be disappointed and discouraged when things don't. But if we believe life is the most precious gift we can have, no matter what pain or loss we experience, we will endure. In recovery, we're learning that life can be good and that our Higher Power and others will help us through the bad times. We're mentally, physically, and spiritually prepared for all that life may bring us. We are becoming grateful for life, our blessings, and even our problems.

Today help me to believe that life is precious
so I may not fear it but rejoice in it daily.

The only way to have a friend is to be one.
— *Ralph Waldo Emerson*

Growing up in a dysfunctional home taught us not to talk or trust or feel. Spending all our energy trying to survive, we were probably not taught how to have or be a friend. But we are learning this now.

Although learning to have and be a friend requires some intense self-evaluation, the rewards outweigh the risks. The first step toward developing healthy friendships is to understand the disease that has afflicted us. When we know why we reacted the way we did, we can learn how not to repeat these behaviors. No longer sick and confused, we are making better choices now, and we are able to act on them.

Now we can find people who have shared our problem, people who can help us break out of our isolation. By attending meetings and talking with our sponsor, we learn to trust again. Sometimes it is hard, because we are trying to change behaviors that have been with us since childhood. But now we have a Higher Power to help us and sustain us.

The friends we have now will last a lifetime. Soon we will feel confident that we can be a friend and will finally feel the warmth we've missed for so long.

Today help me learn how to be a friend.

To be everywhere is to be nowhere.
— *Seneca*

Sobriety has taught us the value of a sense of purpose, a center to target our energies. Too often, we tried to be all things to all people, then ran in too many directions at one time. The typical result was frustration and poor accomplishments. This left us with low self-esteem and even less willingness to pursue healthy goals.

We can apply the principles we've learned in Twelve Step recovery to any area of our lives and steer a more direct, spiritually sound course. We can focus on doing "First things first," and taking small steps toward what we want. It is far more dignified and joyous to arrive somewhere, tasks fulfilled, than to dart about and achieve nothing.

We needn't change everything at once. We can repair our bodies with a modest exercise program, get a little more rest, and add a few healthy foods to our diet. To activate our minds we can take a class or pursue a lost hobby. And to enrich our spiritual lives, we can take a few minutes each day to connect with our Higher Power. By taking small, humble steps, we stay within our abilities and focus on the true direction we need in our new sober life.

Today let me concentrate on each
small step I take toward my goals.

Acceptance doesn't mean resignation—it means
understanding that something is what it is and
that there's got to be a way through it.
— *Michael J. Fox*

Letting go of control often does not come easy to us. If
we pray, we usually start out praying for what we want.
Gradually, though, our recovery program teaches us to
ask not for what we want but for understanding and
acceptance of whatever life brings today. This helps bring
our lives in tune with our surroundings and helps us let
go of the need to control others and the events around
us. It offers us the chance to use our energy for living
in the moment, rather than worrying about outcomes.
And it brings peace to our hearts to trust that our Higher
Power will take care of outcomes.

When we begin to seek acceptance, we free ourselves.
We give up the need to be "the boss" of everything, the
need to be in control, the need to be responsible for
everything. Practicing acceptance and gratitude is our
one-way ticket to peace and serenity.

Today let me accept whatever
life brings to me.

Keep coming back.
— *Program saying*

These words mean a lot to us. They remind us that our recovery program really does work.

When we feel doubt, it helps to think back to where we were before recovery. Our drinking, drugging, gambling, compulsive eating, or starving was out of control. The pain we felt was indescribable, although we denied it at the time.

Now, when someone says, "Keep coming back," the words remind us why we are coming back—to get the love, understanding, and support that we need to keep our lives sane and spiritually sound.

It isn't easy. We often lose track of where we are. We are tempted to go back to the old ways. But we can't. We've had a taste of real spirituality, and we yearn for more. Knowing the program works keeps us coming back for the love and support we need to recover "One day at a time."

*Today help me remember that my life is
so much better than when I was using.*

Order is a lovely thing;
On disarray it lays its wing,
Teaching simplicity to sing.
— *Anna Hempstead Branch*

There is a spiritual quality about the order found in nature. Is there any greater spiritual experience than watching a beautiful sunset, seeing the infinite number of stars in the sky at night, or looking closely at the structure of a single snowflake?

Order in our lives helps us relax and think and plan creatively. We tend to be more serene and hopeful when there is order, rather than when there is chaos.

And when we recognize our place in the order of nature and the world, we begin to have a sense of belonging to something greater than ourselves. We know, now, that we each have a special and important place in the world.

Today I give thanks for the order
recovery has brought to my life.

Lilies that fester smell far worse than weeds.
— William Shakespeare

When something or someone makes us angry and we deny or ignore it, it will become a resentment one day. Resentments hurt us because we suffer, but the person we're angry with does not.

Resentments eat away at us; they make us into angry, negative, short-tempered, or depressed people. The key to preventing resentment is to start expressing our feelings. We can also talk to a third party, someone with whom we feel safe. But we must somehow express our anger so we can move past it.

We do this not to change the other person but to unload the poison of resentment from ourselves. Once we've acknowledged it, we often are able to forgive or forget. We no longer carry that burden. Anger does not have to burn in our hearts today. We can let go of anger, and that feels wonderful.

Today help me accept my feelings
and express them in a safe way.

Glance at negatives, but focus on positives.
— *Maxwell Maltz*

It is always easy for an addicted person to focus on the negatives. Up until now we have had little experience with positives. But now we can learn to use life's negatives as tools for learning rather than as an outline for continued failure.

Taking an inventory will turn negatives into such tools and rid us of the excess baggage we've been carrying for so long. By making a searching and fearless moral inventory, writing it all down on paper, we can see the past for what it was, recognize what caused it, and think about what we can learn from it. Then, and only then, can we dispose of the past.

Our disease has kept us from looking at the positive side of many things. But already we can find many positive changes in our lives. We are more healthy, more emotionally stable. Our minds are clear again. And we have a Higher Power to protect and love us. Soon we'll be able to find joy wherever we look and to realize the value of positive thinking.

Today help me see the positives
in my negatives.

If you pray for bread and bring no basket to carry it, you prove the doubting spirit which may be the only hindrance to the boon you ask.

— *Dwight L. Moody*

If we have been introduced to the fellowship of a Twelve Step program, how can we still doubt the power of asking for help? When we were hopeless and our lives were in a shambles, didn't we ask, wish, or plead for deliverance?

Whether we were praying or not, our prayers have been answered. It doesn't matter if we think it was God or the members of our Twelve Step program or some other Higher Power that came through for us. What matters is we asked and we were answered. If this doesn't demonstrate the power of asking for help, what will?

We are letting go of doubt and suspicion. It is time to remember that even in our day-to-day lives, there is a Power greater than ourselves we can turn to. We no longer have to resign ourselves to suffering. Faith is our "basket." If we bring the basket to carry the bread, we will never be alone.

Today help me summon my faith so I can accept the gifts that await me.

*Blessed are they which do hunger and thirst
after righteousness: for they shall be filled.*
—*Matthew 5:6 (KJV)*

A common characteristic of early recovery is impatience.
We've lived in misery and chaos for so long that it's hard
to wait for our lives to change. And we are spiritually and
morally bankrupt—we have no reserves of patience to
draw on. That is why a solid recovery program can be
very helpful. We can see the immediate results of our
efforts—from illness to wellness in Twelve simple Steps.

Every step of the way, our Higher Power and our fellowship are with us, encouraging our efforts and lifting
our spirits. We find we can turn our will and our lives
over to a Power greater than ourselves with trust. And
with this first act of surrender, we find a new life filled
with tolerance, kindness, and love.

*Today I pray that I will always see the amazing
presence of a Higher Power in my life.*

Appreciate the moment.
— *Isamu Noguchi*

Imagine living in a time warp where everything is slowed down. An hour would take a year to unfold. The events of five minutes would last a month. With so much time, we could look at everything in greater detail. We could see and think about every detail of everything that surrounds us.

Now, try letting time speed up to normal but retain the awareness and curiosity for detail we found in the time warp. How much richer our lives are when we take the time to look around us. Our Higher Power has stocked each moment with a treasure for us. Living for the moment in sobriety helps us become aware of the little joys that previously passed us by. In these little moments we find life itself, and in each found treasure we see the footprints of our Higher Power, always walking beside us.

Today help me to see the beauty of
a flower, a smile, a sober lifestyle,
one moment at a time.

A great flame follows a little spark.
— *Dante Alighieri*

Most of us start our recovery with just a little spark of hope. We're not sure what we'll find but pray it will be better than the misery of active addiction. At first, we're afraid to trust ourselves or others, even those in our recovery program. We may feel like giving up. But somehow we keep that little spark alive.

In time, as we find a new way of life, the spark grows. Soon we're more honest, more true to our own values. We become physically and emotionally healthy again and make good choices about the people, places, and things in our lives.

Most important, we regain our spiritual health. We choose a Higher Power, and with the help of that Power, we learn to forgive ourselves for yesterday and to move toward a healthier tomorrow. Then, as our spiritual growth and recovery become a way of life, we learn again about the healing power of love. We find healthy ways of loving others and feel worthy of accepting love ourselves. We learn to give again.

Now as we look to the future with confidence and serenity, we realize that our little spark has, indeed, become a mighty flame.

*Today help me keep the spark of
recovery alive and growing.*

Information is a virus that carries freedom.
— *Walter B. Wriston*

In our recovery from addiction, we found that information grants freedom. Before we knew we had an illness called addiction, we thought we were bad people. Then somehow, each of us got the information that there is hope, there is treatment, there is a program for recovery, and there is a new life waiting for us. We began moving toward freedom—freedom from alcohol and other drugs, freedom from fear, and freedom from despair and self-hatred.

Our minds constantly process events and tell us who we are. As we learn healthy new ways to live, our minds grow in positive ways, too. We find we're hungry for knowledge. Gathering information is one reason we continue to go to meetings and read daily meditations—information helps us remain free. It reminds us of where we've been and where we are going. And we gain new insight into illness, addiction, and ongoing recovery.

Information can bring us freedom.

Today help me stay willing
to listen and learn.

I get angry about things,
then go on and work.
— *Toni Morrison*

Rage, big angers, and old resentments cause our blood and emotional pressures to rise. There is no comfort or healing in rage against another, only pain and frustration. Nurtured anger has a way of turning back on itself and making us sick inside. Certain cultures even prescribe "forgiveness" as a cure for illness, based on a belief that resentment can make us physically and emotionally sick.

Giving up old resentments may feel like saying good-bye to a longtime friend. It may not have been a happy friendship, but at least it was familiar.

Letting go of anger may be frightening. But giving up anger doesn't mean our enemy was right—it means only we are tired of being bound to that person with pain. It means that we are no longer willing to allow mind, body, and spirit to be poisoned by the venom of nurtured hurt and anger.

And when we let go of pain and anger, we make room for love and joy.

Today let me give up my resentments.
Help me heal and free my energies
for a richer, more productive life.

You can clear the land, plow the field,
spread the fertilizer, and plant the corn.
But you cannot make it rain.
— *Melody Beattie*

Spinning our wheels seems to be part of being human, and it is a wise person who can let go of life and trust in the rhythms of time and nature. We want so badly to control our lives and solve our problems independently—our upbringing and our culture often proclaim this as the highest of ideals. But now we know that control is an illusion. And we remember the times we thought we were most in control as being quite out of control instead.

Paradoxically, we are finding that the more we surrender—the more we let go of our own self-will—the more new doors open and the more choices we have. When we let go, we gain. We are blessed when we come to understand this—when we do the footwork but turn over the outcome. We are blessed when we "Let go and let God."

Today help me do the footwork but
let go of the outcome. Help me
"Let go and let God."

*One of the greatest challenges in creating
a joyful, peaceful, and abundant life is
taking responsibility for what you do and
how you do it.*

— Iyanla Vanzant

We may have come into recovery thinking, "Now I'll find out how to make everyone change!" Only after hard work and determination do we come to understand that we must be the one to do the changing.

We may be willing to change our thinking, but this also requires accepting the responsibilities that go along with that change. Sometimes we will have to accept the hurt as well the happiness. Self-knowledge gives us great power—it releases us from past actions and gives us the power to make better choices in the present. It is up to us to be responsible and deal with change in a positive way.

Change can open many doors in our lives, and we need not be afraid of this challenge. Look how much we've changed since we got sober. Our bodies and minds are healthy and fit again. And with the help of our Higher Power, we've embraced our spiritual selves as never before. All of this came from making one positive choice after another. In recovery, we have the power to keep making changes that enrich our lives.

*Today let me change one small thing in me
to make myself a better person.*

Time is the school in which we learn,
Time is the fire in which we burn.
— *Delmore Schwartz*

When our lives were out of control, we often tried to burn the candle at both ends, staying up late drinking or drugging and then trying to hold down a job that required us to get up early. When it came to choosing between the two, we often chose our addiction and called in sick the next day. We made other unhealthy choices, too. We often chose our addiction over loved ones, regular meals and exercise, and prayer and meditation.

Now we make new choices. We have the same amount of time we always did, but we seem to get more done and still have time for relaxation, sleep, and play. We have time for other people and our Higher Power. As we live our lives in recovery, we are discovering something we never expected—that we never stop learning and that life does get better as we grow older—as long as we grow.

Our time in this life is limited, but when we live lovingly in the present, we make the most of every day, growing in strength, wisdom, and love.

Today help me choose health each moment
and do what needs to be done.

The firmest friendships have been found in
mutual adversity, as iron is most strongly
united by the fiercest flame.
— *Charles Caleb Colton*

No one is immune from addiction or its effects—addiction is an equal opportunity disease. So, our fellowship attracts all kinds of people, and we probably won't like every person who walks through the door. But all of us, because we did walk through that door, have a common bond.

All of us faced the seemingly impossible task of turning away from active addiction—and all of us chose recovery over death. We all suffered losses we thought we'd never recover from. But in these rooms, with the help of each other and our Higher Power, we do recover. All of us have struggled to combat self-hatred, shame, and crippling guilt. We still struggle, even today, but we fight the battle with help from each other.

Our bond is one of suffering and hope, a spiritual link that is strong enough to carry us for the rest of our lives in recovery. As different as we all are, our fellowship makes us one.

Today help me be grateful for my
recovery and the fellowship that has
brought me to this place.

Well done is better than well said.
— *Benjamin Franklin*

How many times have we told ourselves we're going to do something—exercise, write a letter, paint the house, quit drinking—but never get around to it? Those around us may have been very impressed with our good intentions, happy we had made a decision to do something. But as time went by and we didn't do anything, they were less and less impressed. Finally, our most sincere promises fell on deaf ears. People no longer believed us. And no wonder. Perhaps we, too, stopped believing in our own good intentions. Some of us may have wondered if we'd ever follow through.

But there is good news. Today, we're not telling ourselves that one of these days we'll do something about our drinking or using or eating. We're in recovery. And we're seeing real progress, real growth in our lives. We're regaining what we thought was lost forever. We've taken the first step toward real, lasting change. In time, we'll find we can make good on our good intentions and rebuild our trust in ourselves.

Today let me feel grateful for the
program. Let me see how it has
already helped me change.

*To me, spirituality is taking a bath
while reading* People Magazine.
— *Laura Davis*

Feeding our spirit can be an adventure in originality.
There are no rules that tell us where and how to meet
our deepest spiritual needs. Our Higher Power can be
found in a rainstorm, supermarket, or temple. Perhaps
an ability to slow down lays the foundation for grace
and fulfillment.

Our Higher Power seems to be closest to us when we
relax and let ourselves, other people, and life just be.
Stress and worry can block our spiritual channels. What
a wonderful opportunity to find ways to relax with a deep
"Let go," opening us up to layers of peace and renewal.

When we have trouble with our spiritual connection,
perhaps we need to look for our Higher Power in everyday life, even in relaxation and fun.

*Today I will look for my Higher Power
in new places.*

*Paying careful attention both to what I need
and to what I can offer up, I become a part
of the human community.*

— Marya Hornbacher

Sometimes we find ourselves wanting things to be different right away. When that doesn't happen, we may feel angry and upset that our needs are not being met, our wishes not fulfilled.

Now we're learning that change doesn't come from outside us but from within. When we're looking for kindness and compassion, we must find it first in our own hearts. When we need order and discipline in our lives, we need to find them within ourselves.

In the beginning, taking such an active role may seem strange to us. But in time we come to relish changing our own lives for the better instead of waiting for change to happen. Our Higher Power is always waiting to grant us comfort and support. New things are there for us to learn. Our Twelve Step fellowship has advice, friendship, and love for the asking. We have the time and the tools to rebuild our physical strength.

We are not alone. And we are not helpless. We're learning to look forward to a new and exciting way of life—"One day at a time."

Today help me remember to help myself.

*Sometimes when I'm struggling with a
problem, I have to do something else to
clear my mind.*

— *Anna S.*

Tossing and turning, wrestling with a problem, can be
a dead-end street. Sometimes it's better to admit our
powerlessness and do something different. We can listen
to music, read a book, exercise, watch television, take a
walk, pray, or meditate.

Remembering that we're powerless can help with day-
to-day problems, too. We're powerless over other people's
behavior and over their reactions to us, powerless over
the weather, the day of the week, the year, the time the
sun rises and sets.

We're powerless over just about everything except
ourselves. Tossing and turning, demanding we come up
with a solution, is the same self-will we struggled with
during addiction. And this self-will is just as dangerous
with little problems as it was during our active addiction.

But we have new choices now. Thanks to our recovery
program, we can turn our thoughts and energies over to
our Higher Power and our Twelve Step program. We can
let go with trust and serenity.

*Today give me the strength to let go.
Grant me the sense to know when
enough is enough.*

*The best thing for being sad is to learn
something. . . . Look what a lot of things
there are to learn.*

— *T. H. White*

Boredom can be a real problem in recovery. We may spend too much time thinking about ourselves and not enough time thinking about other things. A whole world of knowledge is there for us, ours for the taking.

A seventy-seven-year-old man told his group that he'd recently taken up painting with watercolors. He'd never touched a brush before in his life but thought it might be fun. He got some inexpensive paper, borrowed a few books from the library, and gave it a try. Every sunny morning he went to the park and painted pigeons or squirrels, people walking by, or trees, thoroughly enjoying himself. He soon discovered he could have the time of his life doing something new, learning as he went.

That man knew an important secret about life. When we're feeling down or depressed, feeling that our lives are worn out and over, we can do something different, try something new, learn something, take a chance. Our minds brought us this far in recovery, and a whole world is there for us, if only we reach out for it.

*Today help me remember all my choices
and take advantage of all that
life has to offer.*

Nobody's family can hang out the sign,
"Nothing the matter here."
— *Chinese proverb*

While we were drinking and using, we often found it easy to judge others. It made us feel better to say, "Those people have a lot of problems. I'm glad I'm not like them."

Today, we are much less likely to judge others. We are focused on our own lives now. We are busy getting back in shape mentally, physically, and spiritually. We don't have much time—or much need—to be taking an inventory on other people.

And we have learned the benefits of empathy and sympathy with others. Instead of criticizing, we are learning how to reach out and understand others. As we learn to trust ourselves and our feelings, we find we don't need to hide behind a wall of selfishness. Now, we are learning the spiritual value of hearing and helping others. As the Twelfth Step reminds us, we keep our program by giving it away.

Today let me be sensitive to the plight of others.
Help me not to judge those in need.

OCTOBER

Nobody hates a proud man
more than a proud man.
— *Anonymous*

All of us have run into someone at one time or another whom we dislike immediately. We may be repelled by what we perceive as that person's arrogance, dishonesty, or aggressiveness. Maybe we couldn't put our finger on what it was we disliked, but we knew there was something.

Often, what we like or dislike in people upon first meeting them are traits we have in ourselves. If it's something we dislike in ourselves, we are likely to dislike it in others, too. If we take a moment to reflect on this when we have a strong reaction to other people, we may find that what we have is not so much an obstacle as an opportunity. Instead of focusing on the trait in another, we can focus on that part of ourselves, honestly own it, and begin to work to improve. When we have rid ourselves of a personality defect, or are honestly aware of it and working on it, we find that these things in others don't bother us anymore. We're coming to see how self-forgiveness leads naturally to forgiveness of others.

Today I will look into the mirrors
my Higher Power provides for me
to truly see myself.

You can't let praise or criticism
get to you. It's a weakness to get
caught up in either one.
— *John Wooden*

Criticism is a sharp weapon that we have used against
ourselves and probably against others, sometimes with
severe consequences. When constructive and offered
with sensitivity, grace, and dignity, criticism may be helpful but not otherwise.

Most of us are our own sternest critics. To have someone else line up our imperfections and march them
before us only shames us more as it breaks our spirits
and closes our ears. When we treat others this way, we're
left feeling mean-spirited and lonely.

But we can let go. The more we work on loving and
affirming ourselves and others, the better we are able to
give and accept constructive criticism. Each thing we
learn how to cherish in ourselves helps us see and be
thankful for the beauty around us.

Today let me be only a bearer of loving
criticism and gentle suggestions.

*All rising to a great place
is by a winding stair.*
— *Sir Francis Bacon*

When we look back over our lives, it's surprising to see how many twists and turns we have taken to get where we are today. Sometimes the smallest event has ended up determining what job we have, where we live, or what people are significant to us today. Most of us would never have chosen the path our lives have followed, yet we can be sure it's no accident we are here today. Even when we denied it, our lives have been led by our Higher Power, not our own will.

Today we are better able to accept and live our lives to their fullest. When we realize that whatever happens is the way things will be whether we like it or not, we can begin to make the best of things. We can learn from defeat instead of pitying ourselves, and we can practice being grateful instead of arrogant when we are successful.

*Today I will look for the hand of my
Higher Power in everything that happens,
and I will make the best of things.*

Only the brave know how to forgive.
— *Laurence Sterne*

We hold on to resentment, old pain, and grudges to hurt others. Instead, they hurt us, weighing us down and creating a barrier between us and the rest of the world. As long as our hands are full of old hurts, we can't reach for freedom, joy, and love.

The key to ending resentment is forgiveness and surrender to a Higher Power. When we learn to accept others as they are without making judgments or taking their inventory, we can live and let live. We can come to understand that others acted as they did not to hurt us but because it filled their needs.

As we continue to practice uncritical acceptance, we also find we're able to forgive our own faults as easily as we do the faults of others. And soon we find resentments fading, replaced by a new acceptance of ourselves and others as both whole and imperfect human beings. Now we can let go of old pain and make room for joy.

Today help me let go of resentment
and accept myself and others.

I am as free of guilt as I choose to be today.
Whatever I was taught in the past need not
decide my present.

— *Karen Casey*

Some of us live with terrible guilt. We believe we are the source of all problems, that everything wrong is our fault. This is a bit extreme. We all feel guilt at times. Some of it is productive, but dwelling on it is not.

Guilt shows we care. We feel bad when we do or say something that goes against our value system. But to feel guilty about every problem, every mistake, every accident is a sign we expect too much of ourselves. We become paralyzed and unable to change and make amends.

And in recovery, we are learning we are not responsible for everyone—our first responsibility is to ourselves. We are learning to distinguish between healthy and unhealthy guilt. Excessive guilt need not be our legacy. We are humans, not gods. It is our nature to be imperfect. When we begin to accept ourselves and our mistakes as normal, our freedom is within our grasp and we put a halt to the cycle of guilt.

> *Today help me know when guilt is*
> *warranted. Help me believe that*
> *I am not always guilty.*

*In order to perceive the world differently,
it is imperative that we learn to retrain
our minds and realize that we can gain
control over our thoughts.*
— *Gerald G. Jampolsky*

Negative thinking can clutter our minds and influence
all our actions and relationships. Becoming aware of
negative thought patterns is a foundation upon which
we can build a tower of remarkable change.

Our minds are powerful and adaptive. We are finding
that we can change our thinking at any moment, age,
and time, if we are willing. Now we know that we can
change anything in our lives when we begin to change
our basic belief system and end our pattern of negative
thinking. If we don't, all our other life changes will be
built on shifting sand. When we do, we discover that as
we build our new base of positive thinking, everything
else we do is in harmony.

*Today let me become aware of how
much I allow my mind to drift into
negative thinking.*

That is happiness; to be dissolved into
something complete and great.
— Willa Cather

Sometimes we may take our Twelve Step program for granted. It's always been there, helping us find a new way of life instead of the old way of death. It's been such a constant that we may forget to be grateful for the men and women who came before us, who created this wonderful program of recovery and new life. Many people have made our program what it is. Some found a new sober life and were lost along the way, but all contributed to our recovery today.

As recovery becomes a way of life, it's our turn to reach out to those in need. We can be available to newcomers—answering questions, offering friendship, and becoming sponsors. We can be more active in our program—helping to clean up after meetings, offering rides to those who don't have them, or volunteering to visit patients in a hospital or a treatment center.

The torch has been passed. As those early pioneers left a legacy for us, now it's our turn to become part of a joyous tradition of love and support for those who follow in our footsteps.

Today help me remember those who will
come after me in recovery. Help me be
generous, as those who came before
me were generous.

When you can't change the direction
of the wind—adjust your sails.
— H. Jackson Brown Jr.

There are many good reasons why the Twelve Steps progress the way they do, but that doesn't mean we must always think of them as a linear process. And even once we have worked the Twelve Steps, we cannot say we are "done" with them. It is often helpful, or necessary, to return to Steps that we once thought were completed.

Recovery is never a completely straightforward journey. As with anything in life, we must learn lessons and practice skills many times before we really feel we have mastered them. Because we can never know all of the immense valuable wisdom in the world, our journey is never truly over. When feeling overwhelmed with the Steps or certain obstacles along the path, some people find it helpful to return to the first three Steps. This provides an opportunity to concentrate on the principles that form the foundation of recovery: powerlessness, surrender, and letting go.

We can't stay stuck on three Steps forever—recovery necessarily involves movement. But, in times of greatest need, it is helpful to remember that we can always return to the lessons that we most need to practice.

Today I am thankful for the
flexibility of my program.

*I was a tiger on the outside and a
marshmallow inside. In recovery,
I'm both—but I don't have to be
either.*

— Karen O.

When we were drinking or using, many of us were two
people. Under the influence, we were sure of ourselves
and our opinions. But the next morning, we were our
old, scared, and maybe shy, selves again. We thought
our drug or behavior of choice was a magic potion that
unlocked the brave and courageous soul within us. We
were convinced we could never be strong without it.

What a surprise to find those different sides of our personality blending in a new way in recovery. The serenity,
honesty, and spirituality we've found help us choose how
to act according to our values and the needs of the situation. With what we've learned, we can protect ourselves
from people, places, and things that are dangerous to us
and our recovery program.

And we can learn to be open with people we trust and
care for. Recovery has given us the sanity to know the
difference and to handle life in a new way. Now, with the
help of our Higher Power, we can be whole.

*Today grant me the strength to defend
myself and the strength to be gentle.*

Finish each day and be done with it.
— Ralph Waldo Emerson

So often when we've had a hard day we dwell on it for a long time, preventing more pleasant thoughts from entering our minds. Peace eludes us, and we can think only of the mistake we made, the dumb comment we blurted out, the important errand we forgot.

This is a spiritual problem. First of all, out of the billions of people in the world, there is not one other person who is dwelling on our bad day. We stand alone. Yet when we refuse to let go of the day's problems, it's usually because we think many other people will dwell on what we did or said. We think we are the center of the universe.

It's also a spiritual problem because, by dwelling on the past, we ignore the gifts of the present and the blessings of tomorrow. Self-forgiveness is the key. If we find this hard at first, it's okay. Our Higher Power will forgive us, and by asking for that forgiveness, we are learning to let go and continue with our day. This is not hard to do, and the rewards are plentiful: a better relationship with our Higher Power and with ourselves, and the sure knowledge that we're never alone and always forgivable.

Today help me see each new day as a chance to begin again with a clean slate and to welcome new opportunities for joy and growth.

*What great thing ever came into existence
that was not first fantasy?*

— Carl Jung

Many of us used to be great dreamers. During active addiction, we often settled for the dream itself instead of working to make that dream come true. It's true that dreams do come true, but they often require work. Perhaps we don't feel that we deserve to have our dreams come true. Perhaps we tell ourselves it won't happen because our dream is unrealistic. Maybe we're afraid of all the work we'd need to do.

When we have doubts, we can remind ourselves of how much we've accomplished so far. Not long ago we were on a one-way street to destruction. Now we are regaining our health, taking care of ourselves in ways we'd not dreamed of before. Perhaps in working toward one dream we will accomplish something totally unexpected, something we hadn't foreseen but that was inside of us all along. Now is the time for us to step into life's great adventure.

*Today let me have the courage
to believe in my dream.*

*When you're through learning,
you're through.*

— *Anonymous*

Recovery is a series of changes occurring over a period of time. Many people identify the beginning of recovery as the day they stopped drinking or using. That's a beginning, a turning point, but the disease stays with us. It's up to us to continue to learn, to continue to work our program, and to let our new knowledge give shape and meaning to our lives.

We may not have been able to comprehend all this a while ago. But the process goes on if we keep learning and growing in sobriety.

We may be unlucky to have been victimized by a life-long, chronic disease. Sometimes we may feel discouraged as we work at our recovery and encounter new obstacles as we progress. But the fact is that our recovery is unique. By working our program, we can become even healthier than we ever were before our disease took hold. How many other people can look forward to that?

With an awareness of all that can be ours, and willingness to learn, we can find ourselves happier, healthier, and more fulfilled with each new day.

*Today help me be open to change
and growth in sobriety.*

Character is a victory, not a gift.
    — *Anonymous*

When our old, self-centered attitude rears its head, we want our lives to be in order—*now*. It is inconceivable to us that our character needs changing: "Surely my wife is causing my anguish," or "If you knew my kids, you'd see why I drink."

But somewhere down the line we wake up and learn that our character might need a little more fixing than we thought. If we are honest with ourselves, we must admit we can be bossy, and, yes, we like things our way.

But now we're growing serene enough to realize that others have problems, too. The kids are struggling with the same things we struggled with and in a world more complicated and dangerous than ours. If we've been lucky, our spouse or partner has stuck with us all this way, even though it hasn't been easy or the way he or she would have chosen.

Life would be easier if things always went our way, but now we are equal to the challenge of compromise and capable of redirecting our attitudes. Now that we have been given back our self-respect, it's time to give our respect and understanding to others.

*Today help me see my arrogance and
inflexibility. Help me bend to another's
needs when it is warranted.*

Write the wrongs that are done to you
in sand, but write the good things that
happen to you on a piece of marble.
— *Arabic proverb*

How often do we have a wonderful vacation, receive praise at school or work or home, or meet a very special person, only to forget those things when something goes wrong? When we are happy about something, like the food at a new restaurant, we will often tell a few people about it; but when we are not happy, we tell everyone around us. This is a way we hang on to the bad and let go of the good things that happen.

It can be the other way around. Memories are like savings accounts. When we dwell only on negative attitudes, we build a negative balance that can sour our outlook on life. If we spill a glass of lemonade at a picnic, we can blow up over it or simply clean up the spill and go on enjoying the picnic.

We don't have to ignore the negatives and problems in our lives. We need to pay attention to them so we can learn and make appropriate changes. But when we nurture and treasure the positive memories, we build a strong foundation of gratitude and serenity for ourselves.

Today help me to be aware of the good things
that happen in my life. Help me to be aware
of my happiness, however small it may seem,
and share it with those around me.

*You are imperfect, and you're wired for
struggle, but you are worthy of love and
belonging.*

— *Brené Brown*

Learning to enjoy the company of loving friends gives
life meaning. Coming to value ourselves enough to select
friends who give as well as take is a blessed experience.
Knowing that we deserve love, we are able to relax and let
those special people in our lives do lovely things for us.

There was a time when it didn't feel good or comfortable to receive attention, praise, or presents. We thought
we didn't deserve it. We thought that to be loved we
must give, not receive. The very thought of glowing in
someone else's attention and love was an uncomfortable
idea, almost embarrassing.

But today, real friendship asks that we learn to receive
as well as give; otherwise our friend is robbed of the pleasure of loving. The same is true of our spiritual growth.
We must pay attention to what we gain and what we can
give in return.

*Today help me learn to receive
as well as give.*

*History books begin and end, but
the events they describe do not.*
— *R. G. Collingwood*

Each day we turn a new page in our recovery, and we grow more settled in our new lives. As we learn to live in the present, neither fearing the future nor feeling shame about the past, we discover new pleasures in simply living. We don't have to hide our fear anymore; we don't have to suppress grief or shame or anger. We don't have to keep our real selves secret behind a veil of substances.

But we do need to remember. Our old behavior is still a part of us. We may still be paying the consequences for it, with legal or health problems. We may still feel remorse over our actions. And we need to remember that our addiction did not end simply because we stopped using our drug of choice. We could relapse at any time if we aren't careful and don't work our program. We could replace our old addictive behaviors at any time with equally unhealthy new ones that may be harder for us to see. This is why we keep going to meetings. This is why we need our sponsor, our other program friends, and our Higher Power. Recovery is active. When we are working at it, we are recovering.

*Today help me see what work
I need to do for my recovery.*

When they discover the center of the universe,
a lot of people will be disappointed to discover
they are not it.

— *Bernard Bailey*

Things happen every day that can make us angry. If we let all the anger pile up, we'll be carrying around a load so heavy our sobriety might collapse under the strain. But it's surprisingly simple to lighten that load. One way is to express our anger openly and honestly when it's appropriate. Another is to remember we aren't the center of the universe.

When we humbly accept that we share the world with everyone else equally, we can choose to respond with understanding instead of anger. When another car cuts us off in traffic, it helps to remember that roads are there for everyone, not just us. It helps to remember that the actions of others are not necessarily aimed at us personally, however thoughtless and hurtful those actions might be. Others don't sit around and plot ways to make us angry.

Now, by humbly accepting our rightful place in the world—no better or worse than anyone else's—we can work to simplify our lives, reduce our anger, and make room for a growing serenity and continued spiritual growth.

Today let me reduce my anger
and grow in serenity.

*Keep your eyes on the stars, but remember
to keep your feet on the ground.*
— *Theodore Roosevelt*

We all know someone who is truly humble—someone
whose inner calm we can feel, someone whose material,
emotional, or spiritual generosity we may not trust at
first.

If the humility is authentic, it's likely that person has
moved through suffering in a way most of us have not.
It isn't that this person has suffered more than we have
but that he or she has moved through the pain—felt it,
expressed it, and let go of it—rather than going around
it, medicating it, denying it, or minimizing it.

We may wish to become people like this, yet we fear
it. By their very being, humble people challenge us to be
present in our lives, much as animals are. A cat is always
fully itself, but we may be only 30 or 80 percent ourselves
at any given time.

We cannot take lessons in humility. It is a quality that
emerges in its own time during the course of our recovery. But as we become more authentic and more connected with ourselves, with others, and with our Higher
Power, humility follows.

*Today help me be present with myself and
so learn what it means to be humble.*

Don't just do something, stand there!
— *Martin Gabel*

We used to spend all our time running around with no time, it seemed, for the important things. Our addiction kept us in this state of turmoil, and we didn't have time for the most important thing of all—our own lives. In reality, this frenzy of activity was an energy-consuming tactic that let us avoid awareness of our addiction. Unlike healthy physical activity, it drained us of strength but gave back nothing in return.

Now we have time to devote to ourselves. This means spending quiet time rewarding ourselves for tasks well done. It also means we have time for physical activity that strengthens and invigorates us—playtime. We might not feel we're ready to take on a regular program of jogging or swimming, but we can take time out each day for a brisk walk. The new energy we gain combines with an increase in self-esteem to make us even more ready to take on new challenges. Our new feeling of well-being prepares us emotionally, as well as physically, for each new day. And our sense of accomplishment at making this healthy change lays the stepping stones for more growth.

Today let me pay attention to my need
for physical activity and do at least
one thing to satisfy that need.

Ye have many strings to your bow.
— John Heywood

Our recovery depends on our Twelve Step program and the principles we are learning. But we also need recreation and outside interests stimulate our creativity and personal growth.

Most of us can remember beloved hobbies, crafts, and sports we enjoyed in childhood. For some of us, years have gone by since we last spent time on those interests. Now, we're granted a second chance to rediscover those pastimes that so delighted us as children. Many of them were inexpensive, costing more in creativity than cash— perfect for early recovery when finances are often tight.

Outside interests can give our lives a new dimension of enjoyment. And whether we return to old interests or find new ones, we need only please ourselves. A hobby can help us forget our troubles for a few minutes or a few hours as we give ourselves some simple, wholesome fun.

*Today let me think of how I can
enjoy my spare time.*

Life is short, and it is up to you
to make it sweet.
— *Sarah Louise Delany*

Looking back over our lives, we can often see patches of light and dark, clusters of events that we remember as good times or bad. During the dark days we probably had little faith in silver linings, little belief that tragedy could yield unexpected blessings. In fact, we may have been angry at anyone who suggested to us to look for the good side. And when we were showered with blessings—even if they were right in our face—we probably couldn't see them for what they were. We simply didn't have the tools. All we could do was keep alert for the downside. So much of our attention was spent looking for pitfalls that we overlooked the good.

But today it's different. When we look back, the past is not so shadowy as it once was. There were moments of clarity and focus, especially during the dark days. One of those moments was probably the beginning of our recovery, the moment we began to realize we could no longer live like we had, the moment we began to choose life over death. We are continuing to choose life every day in recovery, and by this choice we are creating a light even in our darkest days.

Today let me find the light in my darkness.
Help me believe that it's there.

It takes strength to make your way
through grief, to grab hold of life
and let it pull you forward.
— *Patti Davis*

When something goes terribly wrong in our world, we may despair, feeling life will never be right again. Some kinds of pain may seem too much for us to stand. At times like this, we need faith that our grief will fade in time and that we can find the strength to bear our feelings until they change. Broken hearts will heal and we will learn to smile again. We will find new friends to replace those we have lost.

Our Higher Power has a plan for us that we can never really know. We will never be given more sorrow than we can bear. With faith in tomorrow's sunrise, we can survive our grief today. Faith in our Higher Power can help us find peace while we mourn our losses. Our Twelve Step fellowship offers support, comfort, and love to sustain us through our darkest moments. As we find new communion with our Higher Power and our friends, we may realize that sometimes, out of our greatest pain, our greatest joy is born.

Today I am grateful for the closeness
of my Higher Power, especially
in times of grief and loss.

Somewhere beyond the curtain
Of distorting days
Lives that lonely thing
That shone before these eyes.
— *William Butler Yeats*

Recovery can be like a curtain going up a little at a time. It opens very slowly, sometimes dropping back down a little, sometimes staying where it is for weeks or months before rising some more.

This image helps remind us that our recovery doesn't always progress at the speed we would like. It is often a slow process, with many starts and stops. But we know that as long as we work our program, the curtain will continue to go up. We have faith that eventually our lives will be filled with the light our program lets in.

We are on the right track toward a better way of life. Whether our curtain is up only a little or much further along, we share with those in our fellowship a common strength, a common goal, and a common destination.

Today let me be grateful for the
others who are with me on the
road to recovery.

Each friend represents a world in us,
a world possibly not born until they
arrive, and it is only by this meeting
that a new world is born.

— *Anaïs Nin*

With friends we can get through the hardest times. When things seem bleak and gloomy, a friend can brighten the day. A friend can tell us a hard truth when we need to hear one and can help us laugh when we need a lighter perspective.

Now that we're recovering, every day is a chance to find new friends. Our Twelve Step program is a great place to meet healthy people from all walks of life, people with all kinds of experience. Once, we might have had a limited idea of who a friend could be, but now we seek out those with our common goals of sobriety and serenity. We find we have much in common with people of different ages, cultures, and religions. We're all recovering and struggling to find new peace in our lives. Together, we can share our experience and learn from one another, and we can enjoy the glow that comes from making new friends. When we open ourselves up to that experience and make the effort, we discover how deserving we are.

Today I am grateful for the new world
of friends waiting for me.

Almost everything will work again
if you unplug it for a few minutes,
including you.

— *Anne Lamott*

Running around trying to do everything for everyone can bring on an emotional collapse. When we act like a merry-go-round that never stops, we risk breaking down, exhausted and worn out.

Energy is a barometer we can use to measure balance in our lives. We get tired when we give to others without also nourishing ourselves. Frantic giving to others can numb us to our own pain and deafen us to our own cries for help. We tell ourselves, "I can put off resting a few more hours," "I'll take time for myself later," or "I can't possibly take a vacation now."

We are the only ones who can choose to get off the merry-go-round and take a closer look at our living patterns. Pushing ourselves to the limit isn't doing ourselves or those we love any favors. We must relax and take the time to recharge, and when we do, life is a much smoother and more satisfying ride. One way to avoid exhaustion is to set aside a few minutes for quiet time with our Higher Power each day. If we are out of balance, time with our Higher Power will often provide the rest and refueling we need.

Today let me take time for myself.

Stories have given me a place in which to lose myself. They have allowed me to remember. They have allowed me to forget. They have allowed me to imagine different endings and better possible worlds.

— Roxane Gay

A book can help us escape, take us anywhere we want to go, and teach us something we want to learn. Distant places, foreign languages, new ideas, humor, great literature, recipes and cooking techniques, and much more are all ours for the asking. It's all free and as close as the library.

During our days of active addiction, we didn't have much time for books, and we couldn't think clearly enough to concentrate. Now our thinking is clearer, and many of us have rediscovered our thirst for new ideas.

Books can help us expand our knowledge about recovery, learn something new, or just escape into a good story. With the help of a book, we may even discover a hidden talent we didn't know we had. Books can teach us to think, tickle us into laughter, or move us to tears. Books can stimulate our minds and enhance our recovery. When we have books, we are never alone.

Today I'm grateful that so much knowledge and enjoyment can be mine.

The weight of this sad time we must obey;
Speak what we feel, not what we ought to say.
— *William Shakespeare*

Letting others know how we feel is risky. There is a chance they won't care or understand. In a Twelve Step program, however, this is unlikely. We go there to be healed and quickly learn that healing requires us to speak honestly about our pain.

When our peers ask us to share our feelings, they have a good reason. They know from personal experience that the most important action in recovery is to talk honestly about what has happened and is happening to us. To maintain our recovery, we need to stay honest with at least one person.

Meetings give us a chance to talk honestly about our real selves—maybe for the first time. We soon realize that our fellowship is not standing in judgment but is hurting along with us and feeling for us. Our peers hear us and offer us their love and support. Honesty often isn't easy at first, but it gets easier as we learn how comforting and strength-giving the rewards are.

Today help me be honest with others.
Help me share my pain that I may
grow through it.

A little neglect may breed great mischief.
— *Benjamin Franklin*

Some of us neglected our families during active addiction. Our pain was so great that we had nothing left to offer others. We retreated into our own world, leaving our families wondering where we had gone. We may have neglected our families financially, too, spending everything we had to feed our addiction.

We may find it easy to fall into the same pattern again, neglecting our families as we pursue recovery. We must find a balance between our own needs and the needs of our families. Our recovery must come first, but it should never be the only priority in our new lives. Financial stability is important, but we need to spend time with those we love.

Asking our families how they feel, and listening carefully to them, can help us regain our balance. Talking to them openly can help heal old wounds and misunderstandings. We don't do this until we are ready, but when we are, it is an important and loving part of our recovery and the recovery of our families.

Today help me recover my balance.
Help me be compassionate toward
the needs of my family.

I love people who make me laugh.
I honestly think it's the thing I like
most, to laugh. It cures a multitude
of ills. It's probably the most impor-
tant thing in a person.
— *Audrey Hepburn*

Laughter gives us a different perspective. It is the great healer of spirits and hearts, and it dissolves barriers between ourselves and others. When we laugh with another human being, we build bridges instead of walls. Laughter helps us close the distance in our relationships.

Laughter relaxes us from the ground up. Sometimes it is only after a good laugh that we realize how much tension we were carrying. It's like putting down a heavy load and sighing with relief at how light we feel.

Laughter even strengthens our immune system and promotes healing. It boosts our self-esteem and emotional well-being.

Laughter is a true friend. Sometimes we forget to invite it into daily life, but we delight in welcoming it back.

Today let me realize the healing
qualities of laughter in my life.

*My forgiveness may not mean anything
to you, but it means everything to me.*
— *Pat V.*

It is easy to assume that the only reason to forgive is to help another person heal. It's true that sometimes we may want to forgive loved ones in order to help them move past an honest mistake they made. But, sometimes those who hurt us don't even want our forgiveness. On those occasions, it's important to remember that forgiveness helps *us* heal too. If we don't forgive or let go, we are the ones who carry the pain, not those we resent. Our recovery program depends on our ability to let go of anger, resentment, and hurt. So our lives depend on being able to forgive others, even if it means nothing to them.

Some of us fear that forgiveness means opening ourselves up to pain again or that it means we have to let the person hurt us anew. That's not true. We can forgive someone and still know that he or she is dangerous to us or to our recovery. We can forgive someone and walk away, never to look back. But with forgiveness, we let go of the anger, and we let go of the ties that bind us to the pains of our past.

*Today help me let go of anger
and resentment.*

In a radical turnabout from our addictions,
we decide to trust that our deep inner nature
is beautiful and true.

— *Thérèse Jacobs-Stewart*

If we constantly compare ourselves to others and carry around an imaginary scorecard, we will never be satisfied with ourselves. Our feelings of value must come from inside us. In the long run, the only way to shake feelings of insecurity is to reach down inside ourselves for our pride and self-worth.

One way is to write down all our positive qualities, no matter how small they may seem, and keep that list for reference. A love of music, a good sense of fashion, an ability to make others laugh, a talent for fixing cars—these are the pieces that make up human beings. Most of us are made up of pieces like these, and our pieces take on new meaning when we share them with others at Twelve Step meetings. Learning about ourselves means learning our positive qualities and gladly sharing them with others. When we rejoice in the qualities that make us who we are, we don't have the need to compare ourselves to another.

Today help me share something
on my list with another.

NOVEMBER

When you are sorrowful look again in your heart, and you shall see that in truth you are weeping for that which has been your delight.
— *Khalil Gibran*

Great loss takes everything from us. But, in time, it gives back more than we lost. By grieving we shed the old and receive the new. At first we find it hard to believe a brighter day will come. When we look inside ourselves, we find only the hurt and remorse. As we grieve, we may deeply resent people who say, "Time heals all wounds." How can they minimize our loss by predicting its end?

In the middle of deep loss, we may need only a hand on our shoulder and a silent message that says, "I'm here with you." Then, as healing begins, we find ourselves filling up again but in a different way. By surviving such pain we come to appreciate life in a new way. Our feelings are deeper, richer than before. We know about loss, and we are more grateful for what we have. We are more trusting of our Higher Power. We find comfort in knowing we found the strength to endure when we thought it would be too much for us. We're learning that grief can bring newfound depths of beauty to our vision of life.

Today I will move through my healing process, trusting that I am being cared for by my Higher Power.

I finally realized my family needs to
understand what I'm going through,
and now I can share that with them.
— Ken J.

During active addiction, we often became secretive, hiding our behavior out of shame and fear of rejection. Our families and friends didn't know what was happening with us, how we felt, or what our lives were like. Now they may feel baffled again about what is happening to us. They may feel resentful or jealous when we spend time away from them.

We must always maintain the anonymity of others in our Twelve Step fellowship, but we can explain how a meeting works, why it's important to our recovery, and what it brings to our lives. We can explain the meaning of a Higher Power and the important role our sponsor plays in our recovery. We can talk about program principles such as powerlessness, honesty, and service.

Talking about our recovery program is a wonderful way to share our lives and our feelings with family and friends. We can reassure them and help them understand the process of change. By sharing with them, we welcome our families and friends into our new lives in a loving way.

Today help me share my recovery
with those who are close to me.

Lay hold of today's task, and you will not depend so much on tomorrow's.

— *Seneca*

Our only true home on this earth is our body, and, though we might have abused it in the past, it is still keeping us in this life. We can reward ourselves for a good day by taking a long bath, eating a healthy meal, or getting some exercise. Our body will pay us back with the glow of good feelings.

We have sometimes been sad or tense or angry and have not known how to rescue a day from disaster. Often the secret is held in the body itself. A walk in the park gives us time to reflect on our many gifts and brings us fresh air and exercise. A nutritious meal helps restore our strength. In our recovery, we are learning to keep our balance, and that means including the body in our healing.

When we become aware of our physical selves, we can become more grateful for our second chance in life. Our bodies don't demand much in return—only that when we are hungry, we eat, and when we are tired, we rest. Our eyes still see the beauty in the world, our ears still hear the wisdom of friends and fellows, and our arms still share hugs.

Today help me remember to treat
my physical self with love.

When one door of happiness closes, another opens, but often we look so long at the closed door that we do not see the one that has opened for us.

— *Anonymous*

Constantly living in the past is as harmful as always dreaming about the future. It leaves no time for making the most of the present. But we can use what we've learned about the past to make healthy choices about the future. In recovery, we learn to look with forgiveness and without shame at who we were. Gradually, we develop a desire to live in our lives today without dwelling on the past.

Because recovery helps us make peace with all the warring elements in ourselves, we can move into our new selves and our renewed lives with greater security and serenity, as a whole person.

We still may think about all that might have been or all that may be. That's useful. But to dream is different than to dwell with anger and resentment, and now we can tell the difference. Now we know that making peace with our past frees us from that obsessive backward glance—frees us to see what lies ahead. Now we can face the future with serenity and continued spiritual growth.

Today help me lay one more chapter of my past to rest. Free me from my regrets.

*Despairing adults seem to forget that they can
now take care of themselves, that they can solve
most of their problems alone.*

— Brenda Schaeffer

All of us were frightened as children. None of us had all
our needs met growing up, and as adults we are left with
the challenge of filling in the empty places. Sometimes
we get so lost in the pain of our past that we bring that
"frightened child" into our daily lives and feel small and
powerless again.

Learning to grieve the losses of our past—and, at the
same time, to claim our power as adults—brings balance
and direction to our lives. As adults we have the ability
to take hold of our lives and make healthy changes. We
are no longer powerless children but choice-makers who
deserve to be happy and have our dreams come true.

In moments of panic and indecision, it helps to
remember that life is different today. We do have choices.
We can make good decisions. We have the resources to
follow through on healthy choices. Remembering we are
powerful, gifted, and resourceful will help lift our spirits
and bring us renewed hope.

*Today let me remember my strength,
resources, and power. Help me move
forward as I claim the life I want.*

We must not allow other people's
limited perceptions to define us.
— *Virginia Satir*

When did we learn to pretend to be other than we were? When did we learn that what or who we were wasn't good enough—that we could never do or say or be enough?

We learned in childhood, as did our parents and their parents as well. Wearing a mask was a habit that evolved into becoming that mask, while our real selves disappeared.

In many ways, our real selves are still untested. But unlike the old days when they'd emerge only under pressure, we now try our real selves on like new clothes— first in a locked room when no one's looking; later, in the open air; and, finally, with other people.

Being who we are is scary and awkward and strange at first, but it is an act of faith, one that builds upon the next act. These acts of faith are the process that is our recovery.

Today help me show my real face,
if only for a moment.

Freedom is not safety, but opportunity.
—*Zechariah Chafee Jr.*

In early recovery, some of us heave a sigh of relief thinking the work is over at last, that now we can sit back and take it easy. We may think things will come easily to us now that we've done so much hard work.

Then we find ourselves surprised when life goes on around us at its usual hectic pace. Things keep popping up—and not always things we like. At this point, some of us give up. We want life to be safe and calm. We feel we're entitled to sunny days after so much rain.

But we can't stop the process of change. Instead, we can view change as an opportunity for growth. Every new situation offers us a challenge, and every challenge offers us the chance to strengthen our recovery muscles a little more. When we feel fearful and timid, we can teach ourselves to be assertive. When we're exhausted, we can learn to care for our bodies so they can carry us in the days ahead. When our lives are too filled with stress, we can learn ways to reduce our load and relax. When we face life this way, we become excited about change. Now we're finding even more peace and serenity as we meet each new challenge with a joyful heart.

Today help me to accept change as part
of the challenge of recovery.

Wisdom is knowing when you can't be wise.
— *Paul Engle*

One of the most important things we learn in recovery is that we can't handle everything on our own. We couldn't handle our disease alone, and we still can't. Sometimes we still hold on to the hope that someday we'll learn to control addiction, but it's a false hope.

We may be tempted to try out some old "slippery" people or places again, thinking we can handle it just this once. Or we may fall into some slippery behavior—being dishonest, a little manipulative, clinging to a resentment because someone "doesn't deserve my forgiveness."

In recovery, we accept powerlessness every day, not just when we first get sober. Recovery is about regaining power over our lives, not over our addiction. This is why we turned our lives over to our Higher Power. When it comes to our addiction, we can't handle it alone, we can't tempt ourselves with it, and we can't excuse it or use it as an alibi anymore.

If we want recovery, we are wise to stick with people who want us to be well, go to meetings, stay honest with our sponsor and ourselves, and ask our Higher Power for the strength to recognize our weaknesses.

Today let me recognize what I can't
handle and ask for help.

*People are lonely because they
build walls instead of bridges.*
— *Joseph F. Newton*

The isolation of our illness can be devastating. And the more advanced we were in our disease, the more isolated we became. The journey back is a hard one, but to wake up in the morning and face the world with friends is a joyous triumph. We reach out to others like us and realize we are not alone in our suffering.

The pain of our illness made us feel separate from others. We wondered how anyone else could feel the way we did. The fact is, we belong to a special group with special advantages: we know the symptoms of our illness and know what we can expect from our recovery. We can talk about our feelings with people who understand what we are feeling and why we are feeling that way. And we have a way out of our pain and suffering—the Twelve Steps.

We need never again feel isolated from others. Our group and the strength we've found from people just like us will be the bridge to our future happiness.

*Today help me know when I am
isolating and give me the strength
to connect with others.*

They who forgive most shall be most forgiven.
— Philip James Bailey

We come into the program with many resentments: "It was his fault I drank in the first place"; "If I'd gotten that job, this never would have happened"; "I'm coming here to make my wife happy." We are angry and we need to blame someone for our pain. And the hardest thing is to accept responsibility for our actions, to say, "I am here because of me."

But now we are here, ready to change. We soon learn that resentments are a danger that could lead us to relapse. And resentment hurts our self-love. To keep harboring resentments will hinder our recovery.

So we take an inventory and share it with someone we trust, and we begin to understand the self-defeating nature of resentments. We are slowly beginning to feel and express our anger. It can be freeing to realize that whether or not we confront the target of our anger makes no difference. We learn that resentments poison us and that we don't want to let them keep us from our Higher Power. In time, with help from our Twelve Step fellowship, we learn how to forgive and find peace in ourselves.

Today help me take one step
closer to forgiveness.

For after all, the best thing one can do
When it is raining, is to let it rain.
— *Henry Wadsworth Longfellow*

We had no choice about when or where we were born, what color hair we have, how tall we are, or whether we are left-handed. And we did not choose to be afflicted with the disease of addiction.

But we can choose to accept who we are, what we have, and what we will do about these things. Each day we awaken with a choice. It doesn't matter if it's rainy or sunny, hot or cold, or if we're rich or poor. All these things are outside us; they are not what determines if we're happy or not. That is our choice. We choose to make the most of our day, to be kind to ourselves, to tend to our recovery. We choose to be loving to another human being, to offer help or sympathy, to interact with the world—or to isolate ourselves.

Life is not lived outside us, but it is determined by the ways we choose to interact with what's outside us. Each thing we do or refuse to do is by choice, and no one makes our choices for us. Living well is a great responsibility, but with the help of our fellowship and our Higher Power, we can gladly accept the responsibilities of the present.

Today help me pay attention to the moment
and to make self-loving choices.

My little children, let us not love in word,
neither in tongue; but in deed and in truth.
—*1 John 3:18 (KJV)*

We are learning to break the cycle of addiction. By going into recovery, we are assuring that we will pass on much less dysfunction to our children. They will benefit from our new lives and the changes we are making. Now, we have become healthy role models, helping our children live better lives.

It is exciting to think that each successive generation will benefit from the recovery in our families today. Future children will be raised in families where active addiction has been replaced by more openness, honesty, clear thinking, and real communication. We can take pride in knowing that today's work, today's meeting, and today's recovery will pay dividends for generations to come. In the meantime, we ourselves are living in the present with gratitude and healthy pride, choosing each day to affirm life.

Today let me show gratitude that recovery
has benefits not only for my family but
also for future generations.

*The best way to secure future
happiness is to be as happy as
is rightfully possible today.*
— *Charles William Eliot*

How many of us have let today slip through our fingers because we were busy worrying about tomorrow? Maybe we thought that learning how to live for today is irresponsible. But it's not. In learning how to put our best foot forward and enjoy the pleasures of the present moment, we learn that worrying about the uncertainties of tomorrow is of little value. To miss experiencing the present moment is to miss our lives.

This is a hard lesson to learn, but in recovery, we see the importance of living one day at a time. Slowly but surely the uncertainty of the future seems less important than it used to be. By learning to be the best we can be right now, we can accept whatever life throws our way with serenity. Our Higher Power never gives us more than we can handle.

*Today let me be present and trust that
tomorrow will take care of itself.*

Not what we give but what we share—
For the gift without the giver is bare.
— *James Russell Lowell*

Alcoholism and other addictions are selfish diseases. In the past, they caused us to think only of ourselves and never of others. "How do I get out of this jam?" "How do I get another drink or drug?" Addiction is an "I" disease.

Recovery begins with "we," when we identify with others who have the illness and become willing to listen. Recovery works because it helps us out of ourselves: our self-pity, our self-centeredness, and our selfishness.

After we work a "we" program and gain a solid foundation for recovery, we begin to develop the ability to think of others, and the "you" stage begins. "How are you doing?" "How can I help you?" "I am concerned about you." "I care about you."

This is a sign of true change, a sign that our lives are much more open and fulfilled. It is also a sign of our Higher Power's love at work in our lives. We have begun to connect, not through want or need but through willingness to give and share.

Today I pray that I may finally become
able to love and care about others,
that I may be able to reach out.

There's only one corner of the universe
you can be certain of improving, and
that's your own self.

— *Aldous Huxley*

We have given up many things for the sake of our recovery. We gave up our drug of choice, our fear, our unhealthy lifestyle, our addicted friends. We are still giving up our self-hate, our grandiosity, our manipulations, our resentments, and more.

But we can't do any of this without replacing what's gone. This is what our recovery program is all about. We work to replace fear with honesty, resentment with forgiveness, manipulations with acceptance. We are working each day to completely remake our lives, bit by bit. We are replacing unhealthy habits with healthy ones. The difference between these habits now is that we are conscious of them, and we are fully aware of their power in our lives. When we worked alone and lived lives of avoidance and pain, our habits were deadly. These new habits become stronger each time we practice them, and our lives become more open to new growth and change. Now that we are no longer alone, we have picked up another new habit—we are building a life of self-awareness and self-love.

Today let me practice gratitude
for my new habits.

Listen and learn.
— Anonymous

Our recovery program has helped us learn to listen. Before recovery we were focused on ourselves. When we talked to others, our minds were often elsewhere. We learned how to look at others and nod our heads, but our thoughts were really with ourselves.

Now that is changing. We listen to others, especially at meetings. We hear what they have to say. We feed our ideas back. We're beginning to enjoy conversation.

Perhaps it is because we no longer feel like we have something to hide. Or perhaps it is because, when we were drinking and using, we did not want to hear what others were saying to us. In the past, we needed to protect our secrets—even if they were secret only to us. Now we must protect our newly acquired openness.

As we become more open to others, we appreciate those who are open to us. To learn from others, we open not only our minds and hearts but also our ears. In listening to others, we learn to care about them—and about ourselves, too.

Today I pray that I might always be willing
to listen to those around me.

Happiness follows simplicity.
— Irish proverb

Many of us can remember a time in our childhood when we were walking with an adult and our legs were tired from trying to keep up with the grown-up pace. "Slow down," we might have said. In our fast-paced lives as adults, we would do well to heed that child's request—to slow down. Maybe our hurry isn't as necessary as we've thought. Maybe it's a habit from the days when to slow down—to stand or sit still—meant finding out what we were thinking about, what we were planning to do, what our feelings were. We couldn't afford to know that then. Our lives were filled with pain; to acknowledge the truth about ourselves or our situation might have jeopardized our survival.

Today, though, there are things we want to see, things we want to feel. Our recovery depends on it. Besides, we no longer need to use our busyness as a shield. In slowing down our lives, we simplify them, and we can enjoy the beauty of recovery. We look at life through clearer eyes, and there's so much to see!

Today help me slow down my life. Help me
to be happy and enjoy the simple beauty of
rainbows, bluebirds, and sobriety.

God is not found in the soul by adding anything,
but by a process of subtraction.

— *Meister Eckhart*

When we meet someone new and he or she asks us about ourselves, we often answer by saying something like, "I'm a construction worker," or "I'm a nurse," or "I'm a stockbroker." Yet, we are much more than those things. That is merely what we do, not who we are. We are not car owners or homeowners. We may own cars or homes, but this is only part of our real identity. In fact, these things have little to do with our real, spiritual lives.

In the days of our active addiction, we had little inner life except pain. We came into recovery stripped of any identity except as addicts suffering from a disease. We were bankrupt. But now, stripped of things that had no real value, we were able to find a higher purpose.

When we subtract such things as false pride, envy, anxiety, anger, and self-pity from our inner lives, we let in the light we need to find ourselves. The more negatives we take away, the more light comes into our lives. And it's easy to do—all we need to do is turn our will and our lives over to our Higher Power. As we grow spiritually, we will see the results more and more clearly.

Today let me know the real me.

When there is no desire, all things are at peace.
— *Lao Tzu*

In the days when addiction was running our lives, we never got what we wanted from life. We always wanted something more, something different, something better: a newer car, more money, a better job—yet our addiction was working the whole time to take these things away from us.

Now we have not what we want but what we need: full awareness of the present moment. This moment is all there is to life. The past is what we've created from our moments, and it is gone. Only the present endures. If we don't have the present, we are not really alive, and all the cars, money, and plush jobs in the world can't breathe life into us.

Since we already have all we really need, we can begin to find serenity by being grateful to our Higher Power for this. When we are truly thankful for this moment, we will have no desire for more, and we can experience peace.

Today let me live each moment gratefully,
aware of all I have.

*We cannot teach love and be consistently
loving until we stop blaming others and
ourselves.*

— *Gerald G. Jampolsky*

Blame can become an automatic response to the troubles
we encounter in living. The habit of blaming others for
our problems keeps us stuck on a merry-go-round fueled
by self-pity. When we consistently look outside ourselves
for a scapegoat, the blame game can drain our energy.
And when we distract ourselves like that, we are not
taking positive action to change.

We are powerless to change other people. When we
keep holding others responsible for our troubles, we make
them responsible for our happiness, too. Then we are ever
ready to be hurt by them again and again.

When we look at the world through blaming eyes, we
block our own ability to experience love. Love asks that
we gently and gradually let go of the blaming habit and
try to focus instead on what we can change in ourselves
and our lives. When we take responsibility for ourselves,
we find a whole new sense of power, purpose, and happiness.

*Today let me feel the freedom and power
of becoming responsible for my own happiness
as I learn to stop blaming.*

Alcoholism is a disease.
— E. M. Jellinek

In decades past, alcoholism or other drug addiction in a family was cause for great shame. People just didn't talk about it. Families hid their addictions. Most people pretended the disease was not there.

Today it is different for many of us. Although the stigma is still present, it is now much more acceptable to talk about our illness and seek treatment. We can join recovery groups for further support. We can listen to the old-timers, who have such wisdom and experience.

Another great change is that addiction is being seen as a family illness. It's not just the addicted person who is sick but every member of the family. Guilt and shame have been unmasked as forces that impair people's lives, generation after generation.

We are grateful for the disease concept and the understanding it has brought to the treatment of addiction. It frees us from shame and helps us learn to love ourselves again.

Today help us all come to understand
that addiction is not a lack of character
or moral strength but an illness and that
it is toxic not only to one person but also
to the entire family.

I have let go of thinking that I'm the only one who can make the day (any day, actually) perfect, for anyone.

— *Sandra Swenson*

When holidays are coming, some of us rejoice, looking forward to the activity and preparation of the season. Others groan in despair, prepared for too much work and too little reward. And some of us begin to feel depressed; holidays mean sad memories and overstressed systems that will take weeks, maybe months, to return to normal.

During active addiction, we muddled through as best we could. We let ourselves get overtired and stressed out. We didn't eat right or exercise. We medicated ourselves against the possibility of closeness with family.

Now we have the tools of recovery to help us take better care of ourselves. We can avoid or diminish holiday stress, planning our schedule more carefully, keeping some time for ourselves. When tasks pile up on us, we can go to a meeting, call our sponsor, and ask others to take some of the holiday load. As we learn to have healthier holidays, we find ourselves beginning to feel closer to loved ones whom we have missed. We have so much to celebrate now, and holidays are the best time to share our gratitude and serenity.

Today help me use my new life to make holidays a joyful time.

It works if you work it.
— Program saying

The last four words of that slogan capture our attention: "if you work it." Most of the time we do work the program. But then sometimes we don't. We miss a meeting. We skip making amends. We try to change others. We begin again to think only of ourselves.

We know from our own experience that we have to work our recovery program each and every day. We can't just work it on Mondays and Fridays or "when we really need it."

Also, we need to make the effort ourselves. No one else can do it for us. And the best ways are the active ways: reading literature, going to a meeting, communing daily with our Higher Power, giving the program away, helping others.

When we feel like we "have it together" and begin slowly drifting away, if only for a day or so, we can pause and remind ourselves that we need to work our program each and every day. Our Higher Power and our fellowship are always there to support us but only if we keep doing our part.

Today let me find one way to work
my program and stick with it.

One generation passeth away, and
another generation cometh.
— Ecclesiastes 1:4 (KJV)

After we've been in recovery for a while, we begin to see that addiction is not confined to our family alone but is intergenerational, sprinkled throughout our family tree. It may have skipped certain generations, but it almost always reappeared. Tragically, it was often accompanied by unhealthy relationships, mental health concerns, and lifetimes of extreme stress and pain.

We can break this cycle. Although we have lived in much of the same pain and suffering that preceded us, we have a program of recovery our elders did not have. Part of our legacy to our children will be the gift of change. Those who come after us will see something new on our family tree: recovery.

We are grateful to have found our recovery program and equally grateful that we can pass it on. Now, at last, there is a way out. Now we have tools to deal with the pain of addiction. Perhaps one day the pain will be gone for good, worked through by generations of recovering people who passed on a legacy of healing and new life.

Today help me be grateful to be recovering
and to be breaking a cycle that probably
began long before me.

*One ought, every day at least, to hear a little
song, read a good poem, see a fine picture . . .*
— *Johann Wolfgang von Goethe*

Recovery is a serious process, but it doesn't have to be grim or totally lacking in humor. Nobody ever said we can't have fun and enjoy life along the way. In fact, newcomers often comment on their surprise at hearing so much hearty laughter at Twelve Step meetings.

But fun isn't always waiting for us. Often we have to find it or make it for ourselves. But that's an easy job now. Every day has quirky little moments we can enjoy and appreciate, funny incidents that can change our day from gray to sunny. When we're feeling a little down, we can lift our mood by calling a friend who's always good for a laugh. We may be lucky enough to know someone in the program who shares our pain in a funny way. Then, refreshed, we can attend to the serious and important business of recovery. Humor has a way of giving us perspective. We see we're not alone, and laughter lets out tension. We are then able to let in the energy to face what the day has in store for us.

*Today help me recognize the joy
that is all around me. Help me find
the fun in my day.*

A wise man will make more
opportunities than he finds.
— Francis Bacon

Sometimes we are "too tired" when it's time to go to a meeting. We are undecided: should we go to our group or should we take a week off because we "need a break"?

Sometimes we do need time off to get some sleep or catch up on chores. But more often we find an unexpected benefit when we fight temptation and go to the meeting. We often realize our reluctance was really a symptom of a spiritual problem. We were isolating, as we did in active addiction. Old behaviors are always comforting. Often, on the nights we force ourselves to go, we hear something we needed to hear or see someone we needed to see in order to move on to a new level of recovery. We may learn something new or hear some familiar program principle expressed in a new way. We usually leave these meetings invigorated and refreshed and grateful we came.

When we keep our eyes open in recovery and remain willing to go to meetings even when we don't want to, we will always discover what we need at just the right time.

Today help me remember how much
my program brings to my life.

I learn by going where I have to go.
— Theodore Roethke

We used to live anywhere but in the present. Our heads were full of grandiose visions of ourselves, worries about the future, or guilt about the past. We had no direction except toward the drug of our choice.

Life is simpler now. We have a future, one that we have an active hand in creating. When we begin to worry what will become of us, we know we can let go of concerns about tomorrow, do what we can today, and let our Higher Power take care of the rest.

By taking whatever small steps we can today, by living in the moment as best we can, we are learning how to live as we go. What better way to travel than one day at a time, choosing a full, attentive, honest life? Thanks to our program of recovery and the presence of our Higher Power, this is our journey.

Our destination is this very moment. There is no other. With the help of our Higher Power, our friends in the program, and the tools of the Twelve Steps, we learn by living. As we do, our lives take us to wonderful places we could hardly have imagined not long ago.

Today I will take each step
with my Higher Power.

A friend is a person with whom
I may be sincere.
— *Ralph Waldo Emerson*

Most of us were fortunate to have a best friend when we were little. We could talk for hours about nothing and everything. Our friend knew our innermost secrets and loved us no matter what we did.

Somewhere between our youth and our addiction we lost that simple part of life: a friendship based on sincerity, sharing tears, and laughing together late into the night. True friendship has been lost to us lately, but now we have a chance to find it again. We will find it in the fellowship of a recovery group. Our peers are sincere in their desire to help because they all reached out for a caring hand before we did.

Our new friends see us as no others could. They concentrate not on our defects but on our strengths. They share our pain as well as our joy in the progress we are making. They offer encouragement and enlightenment. They offer forgiveness and hope and life.

Today let me be grateful
for my new friends.

*Stress is caused by being "here"
but wanting to be "there."*
— *Eckhart Tolle*

Stress can work for us if we learn to listen to its messages. If we listen, stress can lead us to healing. Many of us have become numb to our own stress and pain. We may have become so conditioned to overdoing and rushing around frantically that a kind of emotional paralysis has captured our senses. But learning to listen to our overtired bodies and spirits takes time, and time may be the one thing we're not willing to give up.

Listening to stress messages in our lives helps us stop in our tracks and give priority attention to ourselves. At first we may feel uncomfortable with the notion of sitting still and listening to our bodies and emotions. We're new at paying close attention to ourselves, at caring for our own needs. But if we have patience and give ourselves time to slow down, we will learn to hear the internal music that tells us what we need to know. This part of our recovery is getting to know our bodies again, listening carefully to it the way we listen to a loved one. After all, the one we love most must be ourselves.

*Today let me realize that I can begin
to heal my stress if I am willing
to stop, rest, and listen.*

> *This is the crux of the artistic process, this translation from the inside depths of our being to an outer manifestation that then touches others, evoking feelings and memories from their own journeys.*
>
> — *Victor La Cerva*

If we are to grow in recovery, if we are to break out of our isolation, if we are one day going to learn to give back some of what we have received, we must find out what our gifts are. That means making art, whether by welding or singing or parenting.

Many of us used to think that art was luxury, that art was for the highbrow elite and had nothing to do with us. But we also used to think that way about having a spiritual life, and now we find a spiritual practice at the center of our days.

Art is not about making a product to sell. And it is not about success or failure. Whatever we make is a mirror. It's feedback. Art is about connecting with nature, our Higher Power, and ourselves. Art has the power to center us, to stop us in our tracks and make us see.

Bottling up our creativity is a form of isolation. By refusing to express our artistic side, we are refusing to explore an important means of getting to know our whole self—body, mind, and spirit. Through art we can find out what our gifts are, and we learn to give them with joy.

Today help me express my creativity.

DECEMBER

*The most wasted day of all is that
on which we have not laughed.*
— *Nicolas Chamfort*

When we first started going to Twelve Step meetings, we were often stunned to hear so much laughter. But we soon learned that a good hearty laugh and a joyful smile are as important to our recovery as all the serious issues we explore.

Learning to laugh is part of our growth. Laughter recognizes our shared experiences and helps us feel closer to one another. It also reminds us that we are able to smile again and that a better perspective on life is returning.

We only have today to live, and we are getting better today, so why not smile and enjoy it? Why not open ourselves up to a good laugh and let it push our pain or sorrow out? Now that we are once again choosing how we feel, we have the power to opt for joy.

*Today I am grateful for my ability
to laugh and share fun.*

That the birds of worry and care fly over
your head, this you cannot change.
But that they build nests in your hair,
this you can prevent.
— *Chinese proverb*

Worry can light on our shoulders or sink its teeth into our flesh. Worry can become such a habit that it may actually take over most of our waking and dreaming hours. Worry can break down our immune system and weaken our natural ability to fight illness.

For some people, worry is a full-time job and life companion. How much do each of us worry each day? This is a good question to ask when we are ready to get serious about changing our worry habits.

Once we have identified how and when we worry, we are ready to reverse the pattern. Progress, not perfection, is the key in changing our worry habits. With an open mind and willing heart, we have the power to change our habit of worry into one of trust. We know as we make this change that our Higher Power is truly at work in our lives.

Today let me begin to replace my worry
with trust and faith in my ability to
use my resources to face whatever
life brings me.

Anything I cannot transform into
something marvelous, I let go.
— Anaïs Nin

Acceptance may be one of the most difficult things to learn, for it means we must give up the desire to control our life and its outcome. Once we have truly received this great gift, we will learn that acceptance need not take away our strength—on the contrary, we will have an inner strength we never thought possible.

When we decided to meet the challenge of a sober life, we took the first step toward acceptance—we accepted the fact that we have a disease, a chronic disease that will always be with us. By accepting this fact, we will be able to cope with our lifelong struggle. This way we willingly accept the friendship of our group members and the wisdom they offer us. They have been where we are coming from, they have suffered as we suffer, and they have felt the hope we now feel.

We are being offered a way of life that, if we follow it, will bring us a peace of mind we may never have felt. By our surrender we are now willing to receive something that is being offered to us—the beginning of a new way of life.

Today let me accept my powerlessness
and any help that's offered to me.

Life is difficult.
— *M. Scott Peck*

Life can be hard, but when we start to feel sorry for ourselves, it helps to remember that it's hard for everyone. All people face obstacles and challenges in life. What makes us think we would be different?

Once we accept the simple fact that we're not alone in our hardships, we discover the secret within that thought: we're not alone. We can feel sad about what's befallen us. We have a chronic disease that affects every aspect of our being. But having the blues is a lonely thing; when we sing the blues, we share life itself with others. We transform our hardships into valuable lessons, and we gratefully affirm that we are alive and still kicking.

We can even be grateful that life is hard. If life were too easy, without challenge and opportunities for growth, without any risk that offers reward, without any mystery that needs exploring, it might be without meaning. We trust our Higher Power not to give us more hardship than we can handle. In that way, problems become a measure of our strength. Handling our problems gives us opportunities to exercise our skills, and each challenge brings us new confidence and faith to go on.

Today let me gratefully accept
opportunities for growth.

Facts do not cease to exist because
they are ignored.
— Aldous Huxley

We may have many bits of unfinished business in our lives. For a long time, we ignored everything but our addiction. But that did not make the other things go away.

Sometimes it seems an overwhelming task to clear up old debts, old hurts, old sources of pain. It's too much, we think. We don't believe we can make a big enough difference in it today. But we can. All we need to do is make a beginning.

By paying attention to old business, we also pay attention to the new. When we begin today to do what we can to clear the slate—by making a payment on a bill or making amends—we are taking a step on the road to clarity, to living in the present, to a life that's less cluttered by old baggage. Each time we cross one item off our list of things to finish, we lighten our load and make room for growth. Whether we are accepting a painful consequence of our addiction or returning a long-overdue library book, we are taking action, showing our willingness to get better.

Today let me begin to clear up old business.

Pain nourishes courage. You can't be
brave if you've only had wonderful
things happen to you.
— *Mary Tyler Moore*

If we feel no one has heard our prayers, perhaps we're asking the wrong questions. How often have we sat alone wishing that our suffering would end, wishing that "just this once God, if You do this for me, I'll do that for You"?

Maybe what we need is not an end to our suffering, but the courage and guidance from our Higher Power to see it through—and the trust that whatever befalls us is necessary for our continued growth and recovery. Though it is difficult to understand in the moment, often we are able to learn from our suffering and emerge from difficult times as better human beings.

It takes humility to accept and understand that our life in recovery may necessarily include struggles, but humility is the doorway to compassion and thus to the loving company of other people. In asking our Higher Power for courage and guidance, we free ourselves to accept it.

Today let me ask for the courage
to endure whatever happens.

*The easiest person to deceive
is one's own self.*
— Edward Bulwer-Lytton

Telling people how we feel is honesty. But when someone says, "I told my wife all her faults because the program says I should be honest," this is not at all in accord with our program.

Sometimes we may twist the meaning and words of the Steps or the slogans in order to hurt or manipulate someone. We may not even realize we're doing it. But this is working against the program, and it won't help us stay sober. When we work our program in a spirit of fellowship and honesty, we don't need to resort to taking someone else's inventory.

It takes fearless honesty to keep us on the path of recovery, and we need the help of others and our Higher Power to recognize when we're avoiding responsibility.

As we come to believe in ourselves more, it is easier and more natural to be genuinely honest. In time we can own our defects and focus on ourselves, rather than on others. "One day at a time," with the help of our Higher Power, we will find a new, honest life.

Today let me focus on my own changes.

This plant would like to grow . . .
and yet escape.
— *Richard Wilbur*

One irony of growing up and becoming mature is it's not quite as easy as we thought it would be. We may wish we could be kids again and have parents who are responsible for making difficult decisions for us. Growing up means accepting responsibility for our behavior and attitudes, making decisions and living with the consequences, and solving day-to-day problems. It really would be nice to have someone else take care of all this for us.

Fortunately, there is a middle ground between being completely on our own and having someone taking care of us all the time. The middle ground is to be interdependent—at times taking care of day-to-day problems on our own but at other times, when the problem or decision is greater, asking other people and our Higher Power for help. Being adult does not have to mean being alone. Asking for help is often a very mature action and will usually enrich our lives with friendship, camaraderie, and contact with our Higher Power.

Today I pray that I may never be afraid to
ask for help. And may I never view asking
for help as a sign of weakness.

I often turn in a crowded city to stare at
a face on which experience has written
a pattern of celebration.
— *Mary Francis Shura Craig*

A beautiful soul can't be dimmed. A soul lit by joy brightens all our features and makes us beautiful beyond measure. Even though our bodies often show wear, an internal zest grows stronger and shines brighter.

Living our lives with vigor and involvement fuels the spirit and keeps us getting up each morning expecting good to come of the day.

This doesn't mean we expect all joy and no sadness. It doesn't mean we don't anticipate challenge. But with each challenge overcome, we gain valuable perspective and learn more about ourselves. By surviving and growing through life's windstorms, we find ourselves more weathered and more real. We also find ourselves trusting more in our Higher Power. Time is teaching us that our surface beauty may be temporary, but the beauty of a joyful spirit is forever.

Today let me value my joyful spirit and
love myself for the light that shines
from my human struggles.

There is no feeling, perhaps, except the
extremes of fear and grief, that does not
find relief in music—that does not make
a person sing or play the better.
— *George Eliot*

How many times have we seen a movie and liked the music so much we went out and bought the soundtrack? Perhaps the music was soothing or fun and spirited. It made us want to sing or dance. It was so good to listen to—it made us feel good all over!

Music of many kinds can enrich the spirit, drive away our worries, and soothe tension. It's a gift we all can have as long as we can hear. And many who are hard of hearing may still benefit from the soothing, rhythmic vibrations of music.

When we take some time each day to stop and listen to music, we contribute to our physical well-being and our spiritual health. And we appreciate it when those who have the gift of making music share that gift with others. We may even find a music-making gift in ourselves that we can share and enjoy.

Today help me take time from the hectic
part of my day and allow music
to heal and refresh me.

I've taken my fun where I've found it.
— *Rudyard Kipling*

Today we've all been given another day to use and explore. Why on earth would we spend so much time and effort on recovery if we don't plan on having fun? What's the point? All we have right now is today, and if we don't put some joy into it, we're at fault. If we're rusty at having fun, we have all kinds of teachers and participants at meetings willing to show us. There is always something to enjoy if we only look for it.

When we bring joy and laughter into our lives, we gain perspective, we lighten our load of worry, and we make ourselves more open and receptive to others who may like to get to know us. We also celebrate the sobriety we have worked so diligently to nurture in meetings and in partnership with our Higher Power. Fun is not only a reward for our efforts but also another step in our healing.

*Today let me live each moment
gratefully and openly.*

I have more memories than if
I were a thousand years old.
—*Charles Baudelaire*

Inside us we carry our entire lives imprinted like photographs. And like photographs, these memories can bring back all the feelings we experienced at the time. They're all locked away, the good times and the bad.

During active addiction and sometimes in early recovery, we tend to remember only the bad times. We created such unhappy lives that it became easy for us to hate ourselves. We seemed to punish ourselves by dwelling only on the bad times, our faults, shames, and sins.

But now we're finding the other side of life again, the positive and joyful experiences of yesterday and today. When we need inspiration, we can tap into all the good that's come to us. Like a photograph, it's all there for us to enjoy again—a special family gathering, a sunset over a church steeple, the face of a special friend, mountains at twilight, the first time we saw our newborn children. It's all there, waiting and ready, our own personal album of positive experiences for us to draw on. It's a part of us that comes back more and more as our recovery progresses.

Today let me remember the good times
instead of the bad. Let me focus on
joy instead of pain.

Believe that life is worth living and
your belief will help create the fact.
— William James

We have a choice today. We can look at our lives as drudgery and the tasks before us as painful and hopeless, or we can choose to take the high road. We change a lot in recovery. We have decided that sobriety is better than active addiction. This decision itself is our affirmation that life is worth living.

Now we are not only beginning to see the real value in ourselves and our lives, we are starting to add to that value. We express and share our feelings now, we have friends who care about our struggles, we have hope, and we have a Higher Power helping us feel at home in the universe. These are all tangible results of the simple belief that life has more to it than pain and the denial of addiction. Each time we act on this belief we add more to our lives.

When we do simple, caring things for ourselves—like going for a walk, taking time for a long bath, or communing with our Higher Power—we place ourselves more squarely in our new lives. By growing spiritually, we enhance not only our own joy but also the joy of those around us.

Today help me create another layer
of happiness in my life by taking
time for myself.

A happy life must be to a great extent a
quiet life, for it is only in an atmosphere
of quiet that true joy can live.
— *Bertrand Russell*

During active addiction, we rarely felt content. Quite the contrary, we lived in constant turmoil. We had no models for a quiet mind, much less a quiet life, and so we lived with a constant noise in our heads, like static on the radio.

In recovery, we learn again and again that our old ways of coping no longer work. They make too much noise, and we don't tolerate the noise as well as we used to.

Now, we welcome quiet. We seek out quiet places, calm people, and serenity in our daily activities. We also find that we enjoy a calmer life and no longer need the quick pace of excitement all the time. We enjoy our daily communing with our Higher Power, and we appreciate our quiet time in the morning and evening.

Today help me quiet my mind. Help me
seek serenity "One day at a time."

*The fairest thing we can experience
is the mysterious.*

— *Albert Einstein*

We've been hurt more than once in our lives. And more than once we've wondered, "Why me?" We may also have wondered why a person we trusted could hurt us so or why someone else behaves the way he or she does. We may wonder when it will all stop and we won't be hurt, puzzled, or caught unawares anymore.

We usually can't know the answers to those questions. We can only choose to let our Higher Power take care of us while we embrace the mystery of our lives. It's enough of a task just to live each day to the fullest without also trying to figure out things we're not able to know.

In many ways, we are lucky. We're alive. We aren't starving. We've found a recovery program to help us rebuild our lives, and we have survived the trials of life so far. What more could we ask?

Now our task is to enjoy life, to grow more fully human, and to embrace the mysterious.

*Today let me accept what
I can't understand.*

*Every moment that I am centered
in the future, I suffer a temporary
loss of this life.*

— *Hugh Prather*

For the most part, we find that leaving the present moment for some future projection leads to frustration. We need to make necessary plans for future events, but idly pondering life's outcomes often converts our present into negative experiences. We lose a piece of today in the process. And we risk sabotaging our recovery by igniting fear and anxiety.

Old habits can be attractive. We used to feel comfortable worrying about the future or fantasizing about it. This was our escape from an unhappy present, and it ensured that the present remained unhappy. Now we are facing life in the present, and, for the sake of our recovery, we can't afford to abandon this moment.

When we remember that this one day is really all we have, live it with a sense of trust, and give it our full attention, we are living our lives to the fullest. This is the ever-present gift of recovery that is ours every day.

*Today let me live my only
moment—the present.*

The sweetest of all sounds is praise.
—*Xenophon*

When we were little and had just learned a new skill, such as tumbling head-over-heels in the grass, the first thing we wanted was for Mom or Dad to watch us do it. "Look at me! Look what I can do," we said. If we were lucky, our parents praised us, and we soaked it up and felt great.

As small children, we knew we needed praise and we weren't shy in seeking it. Sadly, as adults we often pretend we don't need any praise, or we feel we don't deserve it. And even if we did deserve it, it wouldn't be "proper" to ask.

But today we are learning that we do indeed deserve praise, and it's okay to want and seek recognition. If we can't yet ask for it anywhere else, we can always find it in our fellowship. Soon, as we learn to ask for and accept praise, we also learn to praise ourselves and to value our own opinion as much as we do the opinions of others.

Today help me believe I deserve praise
and give me the courage to ask for it.

*We are suspicious of grace. We are
afraid of the very lavishness of the
gift. But a child rejoices in presents!*
— *Madeleine L'Engle*

If we can understand these words, grace has touched us.
By the grace of our Higher Power or nature or luck, we
have been given the gift of literacy and comprehension.
If we can hold a book, we've been graced with hands
that can create, caress, and carry. If we can see or hear
these words, we have eyes and ears that help us know
the world. If we are meditating on these words at home
or in a hospital or on a train, we are graced with a place
to rest and live and be well.

Some of us ask, "Why did I have to get the disease
of addiction?" yet forget to ask, "Why am I alive when
other addicted people died before reaching recovery?"
We'll never know the answer. But we can be aware of the
grace that surrounds us and be grateful for what we have.

*Today let me be aware of grace. Let me
focus on near misses survived rather than
on wishes that didn't come true.*

Faith is to believe what you do not
see; the reward of this faith is to see
what you believe.

— *St. Augustine*

Faith is one of life's intangibles that fires our recovery. Faith is trusting in what we cannot see, what we cannot yet feel, what we cannot yet even envision.

When we were in active addiction, most of us believed in nothing we could not sense. Little by little, because our belief in ourselves was so uncertain, our world grew smaller. We had shrunk in fear.

Now our world is expanding again. Step by step we venture out from behind the walls, some of us only in broad daylight, others taking the proverbial step in the dark. Our faith means we trust the process of recovery, that we trust ourselves just a little, that we trust our Higher Power. Faith gives us everything to live for— because it gives us hope.

Today give me faith in what I cannot see,
in what I can't yet know.

In losing fortune, many a lucky elf
Has found himself.
— *Horace Smith*

By the time we walked into our first Twelve Step meeting, many of us had a long list of the things we'd lost. But what had we gained?

Recovery and the Twelve Steps can help us put our losses in perspective, can show us their good sides. For some of us, drinking or using drove our families away. For others of us, gambling caused us to lose a fortune. For still others, perhaps the losses weren't so visible, but they were losses all the same. For most of us, the biggest loss was invisible, one we were numb to—the loss of ourselves.

So where is the good in any of that? Our suffering has deepened us, revealing our common bond with all humankind, and it has also emptied us of false values—it has shown us what matters. Our addictions reveal us for the truly spiritual people we are. We were searching for something back then, probably alone, with no notion of the consequences. Now we have a second chance to find ourselves, a Higher Power, and the love of others.

Today give me the strength
to continue my search.

Friendship is a sheltering tree.
— *Samuel Taylor Coleridge*

It's difficult to imagine a sadder, lonelier life than one without friends. A friend is someone we can laugh and cry with, get mad at the world with, and share our most secret thoughts with. When trouble comes, a friend is someone we can turn to for help without fear of being turned away or judged.

One of the ironies of addiction is that it tends to destroy healthy friendships while it creates unhealthy ones. In alcoholism, for instance, when our friends stopped calling us because of our drinking, our other "friend," the bottle, always seemed to be there.

Recovery is the time to say goodbye to this and other unhealthy friendships and make new ones. It may be scary to let go because we may not know what life will be like without addiction. It is a leap of faith. The good news is that lots of other people have made these changes and are now happier than ever before. Our Twelve Step groups are gatherings of friends who have a common purpose and goal and are willing to go to any means to attain that goal: sobriety. These friends are there to help us attain and maintain the same goal, "One day at a time." That's what real friendship is all about.

Today help me not take my friends for granted,
and help me be a friend to others.

Life is a great bundle of little things.
— *Oliver Wendell Holmes*

We make progress every day in recovery, even when we are unaware. This is especially true if we suffer a relapse. To many people, relapse could easily be the breaking point, but others of us have come through even stronger than we were before. Where do we find this strength? We have accepted the protection of a Higher Power in our lives and understand that to make progress we must also accept some suffering along the way.

Before we came into the program, our suffering was at its worst. The decision to seek help was our first step of progress. A willingness to accept the help that was offered was our second important step toward health. We continue to make progress every day even when we seem only to inch along. At every stage of recovery, we can be proud of what we've accomplished, and it's important to stop and acknowledge this. Once we accept that our pain can give us strength, we begin to learn a positive lesson from every situation.

*Today let me turn some of
my pain into progress.*

A merry heart doeth good like a medicine.
— *Proverbs 17:22 (KJV)*

During active addiction we didn't laugh much. When we were living in that gray area between life and death, everything was serious. Nothing was worth smiling about. As our addiction progressed, we began to be suspicious and resentful of other people's happiness. Life was such a serious business for us and surely not a laughing matter.

In recovery, we're becoming healthy enough to laugh again. We're getting enough rest, we're taking care of ourselves, and we've found communion with a Higher Power. Suddenly we find how wonderful even a smile can feel. The old angers, fears, and anxieties are put in their proper perspective. We feel younger, more powerful, less burdened by the cares of the world. Now, it doesn't take much effort to have fun. Our Twelve Step meetings are a harmonious mix of seriousness and laughter.

In a way, it's like coming home again to the child in us, coming home to joy and peace. A little laughter sure can do a lot.

Today help me to get back in touch
with fun and laughter in my life.

The fundamental and first message of Alcoholics Anonymous to its members is that they are not infinite, not absolute, not God.

— *Ernest Kurtz*

Regardless of what form our addiction has taken or what kind of Higher Power we believe in, most of us struggle with the fact that we are not supreme beings. We try to maintain control with statements such as, "I have to," "I should," or "You must," only to realize that these words are a setup for anger, resentment, or disappointment.

Although the First Step tells us we are powerless over our disease, true belief that we are *not God* doesn't happen overnight. We have all heard someone say, "I go to meetings and read the Steps, but still everything is not exactly how I want." We want to turn over our will but not if it means turning over our lives, not if it means we can't determine the outcome, as if we ever could.

In time, however, we learn in our bones that we can't believe in anything until we remove the guard from the gate, until we relinquish control. Then our Higher Power takes over and our trust frees us from the need to control. Trust opens our hearts to new feelings of love and gives us peace of mind.

Today help me "Turn it over."

*Surrendering control isn't like riding
a bicycle, at least not for me. I have to
learn it anew each time I do it.*
— *Melody Beattie*

At some point in our recovery, we turn our lives over
to the care of a Power greater than ourselves. This does
not come easy. We approach that point with fear and
trepidation. Sometimes we turn our life over and then
take it back when things get tough. We fight, endlessly
it seems, to avoid letting go.

In the end, we find we are not fighting anything or
anyone other than ourselves. We find that our Higher
Power has been with us all the time, even through lapses
in our faith. Perhaps that is the beauty of the program:
whenever we have trouble loving ourselves, all we have
to do is turn to our Higher Power. And then, no matter
what mistakes we make, we will be forgiven when
we ask. This comfort was available to us all along. We
couldn't see it before—but now we know it's there.

*Today I am grateful for the
spirituality of recovery.*

I am only one, but still I am one. I cannot do everything, but still I can do something. And because I cannot do everything, I will not refuse to do the something that I can do.

— *Edward Everett Hale*

We once heard someone say, "Knowing doesn't keep you sober, doing does." We got the point. Our actions, not strictly our knowledge, will help us stay sober. Recovery is a program of action, of doing something that will contribute to our recovery today.

All the knowledge in the world won't help us recover if we don't use what we've learned. Like good intentions, knowledge is only the beginning. Next, we must do— and not do—the things we've learned to help us make progress in recovery.

It's up to us to put the Steps to work in our lives today. We are responsible for eating right and exercising, going to meetings, finding a Higher Power, and praying or meditating to continually strengthen our spiritual lives.

Knowing what we must do is a good first step. Putting that knowledge into action, "One day at a time," will bring us the joys of real recovery and a new life.

Today help me take action for my recovery.

My friend, this body offers to carry us for
nothing—as the ocean carries logs.
— Robert Bly

Our bodies have silently endured the abuse of our addiction and withdrawal. They have faithfully carried us to the point we're at now, and they have showed us a willingness to heal. Now it's time for us to repay our bodies.

The body is very honest in asking for what it needs. When it needs food or rest, it tells us. But sometimes we don't listen very well and we suffer the consequences. If we store up anger or stress, we are likely to get sick. If we abuse ourselves physically, we'll suffer injury or chronic pain.

By listening carefully to our physical selves, and lovingly giving our bodies rest, play, and nourishment, we keep ourselves healthy enough to continue growing in recovery. Even though it's easy to take our bodies for granted, we must not. The physical self is our house in this life; it is our communication system, our transportation, our temple of prayer, and our means of physical pleasure. The way to find balance in our new life is through letting our bodies participate fully in recovery, just as we let our minds and spirits.

Today may I express my gratitude for my
body by giving it some loving attention.

*Gardening is an active participation in the
deepest mysteries of the universe.*
— *Thomas Berry*

We are not alone. We often hear that, but sometimes it's hard to believe it. Even if we try to communicate with our Higher Power daily, sometimes it seems our words are lost somewhere in a void. When these feelings take hold in us, it may help to look for a symbol of our unity with the universe.

An ordinary house plant can be such a symbol. We water our plants to keep them alive, and some of us even talk to them. And there's a good reason. Plants absorb the gases we exhale, and then they release oxygen, which we need to live. We are in partnership. Our Higher Power's job is to provide the soil and sunlight by which the plant makes its food and by which we grow ours.

With every breath we take, then, we know we are not alone. The universe is by nature a web of unity and interaction. In recovery, we share stories, experiences, and love. Just by being there, by "sharing breath," and by being ourselves, we share in the partnership of life.

*Today let me cultivate my
partnership in the world.*

Follow your instincts. That's where
true wisdom manifests itself.
— *Oprah Winfrey*

When we are in the most pain or feeling lost and confused, we can always turn to our conscience.

Perhaps our parents told us about our conscience
when we were small, but we turned away from it during
our addiction. The good news is, no matter how many
times we have ignored our moral instincts in the past,
our conscience is still there inside us. We just need to
learn how to listen to it once again.

The struggles we face in recovery are made simpler
by listening to the voice within us. All we need to do is
take a moment of quiet and truly listen. For some, this
is a way to hear the wisdom of our Higher Power. For
all of us, this is how we can access the wisdom gained
in all our years of living. Sometimes the answer will be
immediately clear. Other times we may need to spend
some time interpreting our feelings. Either way, learning
to listen and trust our conscience is an invaluable tool
we can use to conquer our problems "One day at a time."

Today help me hear and
trust my conscience.

*Imagination is more important
than knowledge.*
— *Albert Einstein*

When we were children we had hobbies or other activities that were special to us: sports, games, building models, reading, baking, playing with certain toys. In recovery, we often find ourselves returning to these or finding new hobbies. Hobbies give us a way to relax, improve ourselves, and create something—all at the same time.

Hobbies, we find, are as important now as they were when we were young. Maybe more important, because they help us rediscover our inner child and our sense of play and fun. They can help us forget our troubles and relax. They help us focus our attention in the present, and when our worries fade away, our bodies relax and renew themselves. Hobbies are an unending source of imagination, pride, and accomplishment. Whether our hobby is something we do alone or in a group, it gives us renewed feelings of satisfaction and pride as well as relaxation.

*Today help me discover a new hobby
or activity to enrich my life.*

I've shut the door on yesterday
And thrown the key away—
Tomorrow holds no fears for me,
Since I have found today.
— *Vivian Y. Laramore Rader*

Feeling guilty or ashamed about the past—about what we did or did not do, about what happened to us, about who we were—can be our undoing. We must work long and hard in our recovery to work through these feelings. We don't aim to forget the past—for it informs all that we value in ourselves today—but to put the past into perspective.

After we've taken an inventory and grieved our losses, we must forgive ourselves. In forgiving ourselves, we can let go of the past and live in today.

With our program of recovery, looking back is not as frightening as it once was. And today we do not have to bear alone what we find.

A new year, a new life, can be ours. Love and friendship, support, and spiritual growth are waiting for us today. Our yesterdays are over, and we can look to the future with joy and anticipation.

Today help me forgive myself for
what's past and learn to have faith
in what is to come.

About Hazelden Publishing

As part of the Hazelden Betty Ford Foundation, Hazelden Publishing offers both cutting-edge educational resources and inspirational books. Our print and digital works help guide individuals in treatment and recovery, and their loved ones. Professionals who work to prevent and treat addiction also turn to Hazelden Publishing for evidence-based curricula, digital content solutions, and videos for use in schools, treatment programs, correctional programs, and electronic health records systems. We also offer training for implementation of our curricula.

Through published and digital works, Hazelden Publishing extends the reach of healing and hope to individuals, families, and communities affected by addiction and related issues.

For more information about Hazelden publications,
please call **800-328-9000**
or visit us online at **hazelden.org/bookstore**.

Other Titles That May Interest You

Three Simple Rules
Uncomplicating Life in Recovery
MICHAEL GRAUBART

Recovery is hard, but it doesn't have to be complicated. Michael Graubart explains why, when you feel stuck in recovery, there are only three rules you really need to focus on.

Order No. 3655, also available as an e-book

Find Your Light
Practicing Mindfulness to Recover from Anything
BEVERLY CONYERS

Respected wellness and recovery author Beverly Conyers shows us how mindfulness can be a game-changing part of recovery from any- and everything.

Order No. 3591, also available as an e-book

The Promise of a New Day
Meditations for Reflection and Renewal
KAREN CASEY AND MARTHA VANCEBURG

This classic meditation book offers daily readings full of inspiration and wisdom to anyone in recovery, regardless of whether they follow a Twelve Step program.

Order No. 1045, also available as an e-book

For more information or to order these or other resources
from Hazelden Publishing, call **800-328-9000**
or visit **hazelden.org/bookstore**.